TACHYON ENERGY

TACHYON ENERGY

A NEW PARADIGM IN HOLISTIC HEALING

**GABRIEL COUSENS, M.D.
AND DAVID WAGNER**

NORTH ATLANTIC BOOKS
BERKELEY, CALIFORNIA

Published by
North Atlantic Books
P.O. Box 12327
Berkeley, California 94712
Book design by Nancy Koerner
Cover Art by Ed Berland
Printed in the United States of America

Tachyon Energy is sponsored by the Society for the Study of Native Arts and Sciences, a nonprofit educational corporation whose goals are to develop an educational and crosscultural perspective linking various scientific, social, and artistic fields; to nurture a holistic view of arts, sciences, humanities, and healing; and to publish and distribute literature on the relationship of mind, body, and nature.

1   2   3   4   5   6   7   8   9   /   03   02   01   00   99

DEDICATION

This book is dedicated to the memory of Helen Gonzales,
grandmother of David Wagner.
Her life was a perfect example of how to live in communion with All That Is.

TABLE OF CONTENTS

CHAPTER 6
EXPERIMENTS WITH LIVE ORGANISMS ... 89

CHAPTER 7
THE HISTORY OF MODERN TACHYON RESEARCH ... 101

AFTERWORD
HEALING BEYOND ALL CONCEPTS ... 125

APPENDIX 1
TESTIMONIALS ... 129

ABOUT THE AUTHORS ... 145

CHAPTER 1

INTEGRATED TACHYON
THEORY OF HEALING

We believe the information in this book will play an important role in the healing and transformation of both personal and planetary worlds.

Tachyon energy provides a marvelous enrichment for a life oriented toward integration, love, harmony, and cooperation in relationships instead of power, competition, and alienation. Tachyon energy is part of a lifestyle that is healing for body, mind, spirit, and the planet.

Tachyon energy opens a doorway that allows you to connect with the divine radiance and therefore allows you to experience the joy of your inner radiance.

In order to fully appreciate the meaning of Tachyon energy, it is helpful to see it in the context of a holistic healing paradigm.

From the holistic healing point of view, to be fully healed there has to be integration in healing on the physical level, the emotional level, the mental level, and the spiritual level. When all these aspects reach their peak of order and harmony, it is said in the Ayurvedic system that one actually has the potential to be immortal. Another thing to understand is that in the process of moving toward this immortal perfection, we evolve in an upward continuous spiral of order and then chaos to a higher level of order through chaos or disease to even higher levels of order. Chaos is a stepping stone from one level of order to the next higher level. Everyone is experiencing this, whether or not they are conscious of it. Each new level of order is a new level of health. This new level of order may manifest as physical, emotional, mental, spiritual, or social health. It may be any combination or all of them. Chaos only becomes a dis-ease process when we get stuck in the chaos without breaking through to a higher level of order. Being stuck in chaos leads to chronic dis-ease. For example, by living a lifestyle of staying up too late and doing drugs, people often deplete their system and go into a level of chaos in terms of their physical as well as their emotional, mental, and spiritual health. If we continue that way of life, we continue degenerating within the chaos, which will inevitably move us to lower levels of order. We might say to ourselves, "this doesn't feel good, I'm out of touch, I'm not there with my family emotionally, mentally, or spiritually, and I have lost touch with God in this process." When we decide to change this situation and give up drugs and the drug lifestyle, for example, then we create the conditions that allow us to go to a higher level of order in terms of healing our physical, emotional, mental, and spiritual bodies. If we take the insights that we've gained from the drug chaos and apply it to upgrading our emotional, mental, and spiritual life, we can naturally evolve to a higher level of physical and nonphysical health. Our emotions can then come back into order and we can go to another level based on our experience of the chaos.

This, of course, does not mean we are recommending drugs. We are trying to help you understand that the order/chaos/order cycle happens on a regular basis. It is a cycle that can be used to help us evolve. Chaos is one of the greatest teachers. By embracing the chaos we could integrate the lesson into our daily lives, moving us to a new, higher level of order. There is a natural evolution of order/chaos/order. It is only when we become stuck within a chaotic pattern without learning or evolving through it, that we begin to disrupt our natural energy flow ultimately creating stress and dis-ease. Most peoples' lives have a certain amount of chaos each day. It could be that something happens, and our response is to become un-centered, a level of chaos. Instead of just proceeding through the rest of the day in an un-centered way, we could stop and say, "I'm experiencing chaos" and begin to explore its cause and messages. We need now to bring in some unified thinking, feeling and experience. Once we get in touch with the feeling we could pray or meditate which might lead to understanding and evolving the chaos, assisting us to evolve into a new level of order thereby elevating ourselves physically, mentally, emotionally and possibly spiritually. If we stay stuck in that chaos, it will bring us into illness and stress. In fact, statistics now show that every ten years in the U.S. we actually double the amount of stress we experience. People are getting stuck in stress, creating chaos on an epidemic level. Chaos does not need to be a prolonged experience. Our model of moving through order to chaos and to the next higher level of order is the normal process for healing body, mind and spirit. When people are very healthy, they do not spend a lot of time stuck in chaos. They are open to it, consciously experience it and chose to evolve into the next level of order. Working with it this way we call moving through dynamic chaos. Dynamic chaos at any level of our life is an evolutionary key. It is a portal through which we can move to a higher level of integration in the physical, emotional, mental and spiritual planes. And if we have the right understanding to make choices and to take actions that are more readily, it brings us into a higher level of order and health. The key question is, what can we do to enhance our ability and power to not get stuck in chaos and move on to a higher level of order? Do we choose to go to a higher level with it, or do we choose to allow the system to degenerate into disorder?

The use of tachyon energy, as we will describe, empowers us to evolve through dynamic chaos to the next level of order, rather than getting mired in stuck chaos.

Tachyon energy significantly helps us to make that move more rapidly. With the use of Tachyon, we are presenting not only a full holistic model of healing, but a process by which we can each move toward radiant health. In this state there is a free flow of energy through the entire body, mind, and spirit that results in a continuous experience of well-being in every moment independent of the outer world. The human energy system is a dynamic system. We must be continually supplied with energy, and a substantial source of the energy needed by humans is assimilated through the subtle energy systems of the body. One of these subtle energetic systems is called the chakra system.

The chakras are a series of vortices located in seven regions of the physical body: crown or top of head; third eye, located between the eyes on the brow; throat; heart; solar plexus; sexual area; and perineal area, located near the end of the coccyx and one inch in front of the anus.

In nature everything has its own self-contained vertical energy structure. This vertical structure, although independent, is also interconnected with all local vertical structures, humans and earth. When we are born our chakra system resembles this vertical energy system. It is vertical and connected to All That Is. Currently, when people grow up in our society, the chakra system loses its verticality and alignment with the ordered flow of life-force energy. In all religions and spiritual processes there exists a description or explanation outlining our separation from God. One example is described in Christianity as the fall from grace. There are many different viewpoints on why and when this happened. At this point it is enough just to acknowledge that it happened and focus on the effects of the hori-

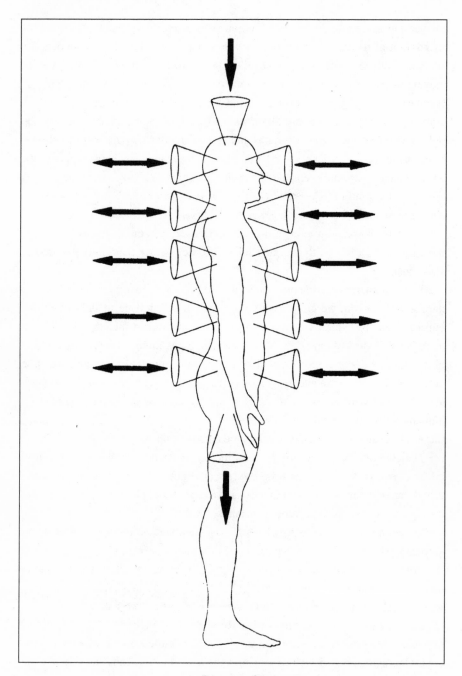

Diagram 1.
This diagram shows a horizontal system

zontal energy system. The horizontal energy system is fragmented, and normally all but the crown and root chakra become horizontal (see figure of horizontal human being). In the process of becoming horizontal, we lose part of our natural connection with the energetic flow of nature. The horizontal shift decreases the quantity of energy flowing through the chakra system and therefore into the body.

This decreased energy in our body creates a subtle shift in which we unconsciously begin to seek to increase our energy from outside forces. There are several healthy ways to enhance our energy, including nurturing our bodies with live foods, pure water, sunlight, meditation, and taking in the elemental energies of the air, earth, water, and sunlight. Association with like-minded people is also very helpful.

In our social world there are several unhealthy ways of enhancing our energy. One common way to get energy is to unconsciously steal it from other people. This is normally done as destructive competition or plain usurpation. These practices are most obviously seen in the business world. For example, if two businessmen or women enter into a discussion, each presents his or her case in a way that seeks to make them superior to the other, usurping the other's energy. This process goes back and forth until there is a winner and a loser. The loser is depleted; the winner is energized. The loser may begin to scan the horizon for the next situation. If it isn't found, then his or her family may become the unfortunate providers of the needed energy. And what if the spouse also is drained? The cycle is unfortunate and unnecessary. When this is extrapolated to the global level, it supplies the social theory to explain the resistance to global peace and it also serves as the source of all planetary atrocities.

The need to feel superior and to dominate an individual or a society is a dominator's way of increasing energy. This is shortsighted because it creates and strengthens a block in the natural flow of the life force. Dominators may appear to increase energy for one person or one type of society, but it ultimately decreases it for everyone. The reason for this is that the energy is stolen and is not in a natural continual flow that connects the person or society to All That Is. Usurping energy from others is associated with a dominator approach, versus the partnership way of being in the world, which adds to each person's energy.

Through the use of specialized Tachyonized™ materials and techniques it is possible to shift from a needy, horizontal energetic system to a vertically aligned partnership system of being connected to the divine source of All That Is. When one becomes vertical, one receives a constant flow of energy feeding the emotional, mental, physical, and spiritual bodies. This is our natural way of being.

When a businessperson is vertical, he or she is in a partnership/cooperative mode that enhances everyone's energy. This ultimately eliminates the need to win at the expense of others. Such people tap into the natural order/chaos/order process, thus allowing the creation of balanced solutions that work for everyone. These remarkable individuals become icons in their circle of peers as someone who is always present, fair, and respectful. These individuals, by their vertical nature, never deplete a situation. They are a source of harmonizing energy, healing and balancing the world by just being. They become natural leaders in the movement toward peace and harmony, regardless of their profession.

The healing or evolution of chaos into order creates harmony. We may work with people and even compete in a way that is enhancing and synergistically improving what we are doing based on mutual growth by valuing each other's ideas. This actually creates a healing or another level of order in terms of how to be in the world. The understanding of order/chaos/order is not just on the physical plane of dis-ease, but clearly includes the mental, emotional, and spiritual planes. By reestablishing our vertical connection, we can move out of domination into harmonic partnership without taking energy from each other but instead adding energy to each other. This shift helps the move to a higher level of order.

As we go a little deeper into the paradigm of holistic health we see that the harmony and healing of the body, the emotions, and the mental and spiritual levels are based on an energy source that is primordial to our existence. Healing at every level is very dependent on tapping into the primordial cosmic energy, which is the source of existence. So the deepest level of holistic healing, and even of maintenance and rejuvenation, is made possible by our ability to tap into this cosmic energy that energizes and creates the form of all material existence as we know it. It is at this deeper level that we can begin to appreciate and integrate the meaning of Tachyon energy as the new paradigm in holistic healing.

Tachyon energy is the bridge to higher and higher amplitudes of cosmic energy that can power our healing, rejuvenation, and return to verticality. This is really the secret of the whole thing. It is the secret to spontaneous healing; it is the secret to all such miracles. We all have the potential to link into or directly attune to this higher primordial energy. Some people may call the energy God; some people may call it cosmic energy; science calls it Zero-Point energy.

To further understand this primordial energy it really helps to merge science and holistic healing by using the language that science uses in talking about it. So we will now talk about this primordial energy as science does by calling it Zero-Point energy.

ZERO-POINT ENERGY

In order to understand the integration of the physical and the pure energy world, we need to develop a theory of how material existence comes into being. Such great people as Einstein and Nikola Tesla spent a lot of time on this subject, and many of their theories are included in the new physics and quantum mechanics thinking. The theory basically states that our body exists "as a precipitation out of an invisible unbounded totality of perfect order." This unbounded perfect order has been called by several names: virtual energy, Zero-Point energy, vacuum state, or ether are some examples. Modern physics has chosen to refer to this energy as Zero-Point energy in a further attempt to unify these theories.

Zero-Point Physics and SOEFs

The world of science has been proving that matter is simply the condensation of a vibrating universal subtle energy substratum, which is the virtual state otherwise known as zero-point energy. In the production of matter, zero-point energy simply condenses into Tachyon energy, which is then converted into frequencies by the SOEFs (subtle organizing energy fields), creating all varieties of forms. The term "SOEF" is described by Dr. Gabriel Cousens in his book *Spiritual Nutrition and the Rainbow Diet*, which explains how this subtle energy organizes and increases physical energy as it moves into the material form. It gives us insight into how it is ordered in the physical body. This, of course, is our concern when we are talking about physical healing.

As the condensation of a vibrating universal subtle energy substratum, or a virtual state or vacuum in a matrix of time and space, matter is made of particular forms and densities of energy. In other words, matter is the manifest structure of all of nature and the laws governing all physical phenomena. In spiritual terminology, pure consciousness, cosmic energy, and universal prana are terms analogous to this perfectly orderly unmanifested state. SOEFs are an attempt to describe how this precipitation from subtle energy to material form takes place and how it is ordered.

Science calls the potential energy, which fills the cosmos, zero-point energy. Zero point exists prior to the materialization of an object. Adam Trombley, an astrophysicist and expert in zero-point technology, said during a personal interview that the materialization of an object in space represents one quadrillionth of the energy available in that volume of space. It is from this state of zero-point, or virtual energy, that we, as a precipitation of this energy, come into existence in a physical form. The zero-point energy in one cubic centimeter of space is said to

7

equal the energy available in a million, million tons of uranium. This is virtually limitless energy. The U.S. Department of Defense acknowledged the existence and potential importance of zero-point technology when it sent out a program solicitation in 1986 which included an interest in esoteric energy sources for propulsion, including zero-point quantum dynamic energy of vacuum space.

Zero-point energy is omnipresent; it permeates the entire universe. It also exists in infinite quantity; that is, it can never be exhausted. There are three characteristics of zero-point energy, which are of paramount significance for us in our world: The first is that zero-point energy contains all potential. Within zero-point energy is everything needed to create perfect form. The second characteristic of zero-point energy is that it is formless and unmanifested. The third characteristic of zero-point energy is that it is omnipresent in the universe. In summary: zero-point energy is omnipresent in the universe, it permeates everything, it exists in infinite quantity, it is completely inexhaustible, and it contains all the potentials of perfect form.

The first stepping-down of this formless, unmanifested zero-point energy is into Tachyon energy. The outstanding German researcher Hans Nieper described Tachyon as a slightly contracted form of energy, or of the virtual state trying to become a particle. It exists at the interface of energy and matter. Philip Callahan, an entomologist who developed the first experimental evidence of Tachyons by hooking a weeping fig plant up to a special electromagnetic sensing device, defines a Tachyon as a particle moving faster than the speed of light. The energy then continues to be stepped-down and patterned into material forms. It also interacts in various energetic ways with material forms. This interplay of research and theory provided the Subtle Organizing Energy Field matrix for Dr. Cousens' theory as outlined in his book:

> . . . these are fields, which both create and energize the template form of living systems. SOEFs exist throughout all aspects of the energetic continuum. As SOEFs emerge out of the virtual state, they are capable of organizing on any level of the human body, from cellular structure to the organ systems, and even to subtle bodies. These SOEFs resonate with the unlimited virtual state energy, transferring it through various step-down systems that eventually transude it into the energy fields of the human body. The SOEFs thus resonate with and energize the body-mind complex.

Zero-point energy is omnipresent; thus we are always resonating to some extent with this cosmic energy. Most of the time we have only indirect or brief experiences of this, but at certain stages of spiritual evolution it is possible to experience this resonance in direct attunement, consistently and consciously. For many, this sort of experience first happens in meditation. As we become more aware of and resonant with this virtual energy state, our minds merge and identify with this awareness as the unchanging truth and the reality of our existence. The resonance becomes part of our conscious awareness in our everyday activities. Eventually, it becomes a continual awareness and attunement with the cosmic energy. This is known as cosmic consciousness.

By increasing the tachyon energy in our lives, we directly increase our resonance with the zero-point energy. We therefore improve all levels of body, emotion, mind and spiritual health and enhance the process of moving to higher levels of order in our lives. This accelerates the healing and spiritual evolutionary process for ourselves.

There is another important ramification of zero-point energy physics that is relevant to our new holistic health paradigm. It is called the theory of conservation of energy. This theory explains how entropy can be reversed and biological transmutation can take place in the human system without breaking any fundamental laws. With this theory as one of our building blocks, we are able to develop a new holistic healing model—a model that explains how the unlimited, formless zero-point energy condenses into tachyon energy form, which is then converted into specific frequencies by the SOEFs. This energy is transduced into the human body in a way that reverses entropy and therefore reverses aging.

Current modeling of tachyon in the scientific world, as described by Ernst Wall, in his book *The Physics of Tachyon*, supported our research and concepts. In simplified physics terms we will explore the beginning, expansion, and evolution of the lepton family of particles. This family includes the pion, the muon, and the electron. The first elementary particle in the lepton family is the pion. The pion exists below the speed of light and has a consistent mathematically computable orbit, which we call the SOEF. All SOEFs exist just below the speed of light and are directly responsible for converting Tachyon energy into frequencies required to evolve, organize, and create perfect form. Of course, all forms are comprised of different frequencies. The SOEFs convert tachyon energy into the particular frequencies needed by that SOEF's particular form. In this case, the SOEF we're examining holds the pion in its orbit. The pion's SOEF, existing just below the speed of light, interacts with the faster-than-light tachyon. As the tachyon energy is converted into the pion's frequency by the SOEF, the pion evolves in an instant into a muon. The new muon has a SOEF (orbit) that is ten times larger than that of

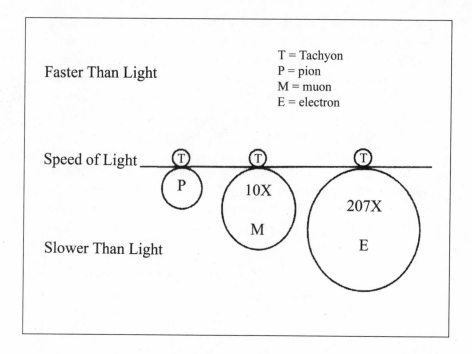

a pion. The muon's SOEF still exists just below the speed of light. As the SOEF of the muon interacts with Tachyon energy, the SOEF orbit once again expands, and the muon evolves in an instant into an electron. This new electron has a SOEF orbit that is now 207 times larger than that of the muon's. This continual process of the SOEFs converting Tachyon energy into the needed frequencies does not stop here, of course, but continues all the way down through the energetic continuum. It continues until the perfect form is ultimately reached, whether it is a human being or any other form that we know of. Tachyon energy is the binding energy of the universe and is responsible for the creation of all forms on the planet. Tachyon energy is the key element in the flow of energy from the infinitely formless all the way down to the perfect form. This flow we call the energetic continuum.

As with all forms in our slower-than-light universe, SOEFs cannot exceed the speed of light. This is a very important point. Our world is a world of form, so the only way for us to interface with formless zero-point energy is through tachyon. The condensation of zero-point energy moves from the unlimited formless zero-point energy into tachyon energy, which is the step prior to slowing to the speed of light. The tachyon energy at this point is moving faster than the speed of light and is prior to all frequencies. Tachyon has no frequency, and as a faster-than-light energy obviously has no spin, vibration, or oscillation yet contains the potential of all frequencies. From a scientific point of view, only frequencies manifest a spin or oscillation. Tachyon energy is the energetic bridge between Zero-Point energy and the SOEFs. The SOEFs are in direct communion with tachyon energy on all levels. It is through the SOEFs that the tachyon energy is converted into all levels of frequencies and forms.

Tachyon energy is therefore the critical factor which energizes the SOEFs. So the more Tachyon energy we bring into our lives, the more energized and therefore organized are our SOEFs. The energizing of the SOEFs is what creates health and rejuvenation because it reverses entropy, or aging. When tachyon energy is free-flowing, we have an endless source of energy to rebuild and maintain our SOEFs, so we continually reverse entropy. This explains how the body can, in effect, become a "faster-than-light energy" conduit, since we are linked to the unlimited zero-point energy as our ultimate source of energy. As a result, the body-mind complex becomes more clear and balanced in spiritual evolution, and it becomes an increasingly better transducer and conductor of energy. As this happens, the body is able to store and transmit greater and greater amounts of this higher energy. This process can account for some of the many miracles said to occur in the presence of spiritual masters. For example, spontaneous healing occurred when people simply touched the robe of Jesus. We now understand that there was a flow of this pure cosmic or God energy into people that reorganized and reenergized their SOEFs, allowing the dis-ease processes to be reversed. People's faith allowed them to draw and be receptive to the healing energy.

SOEFs have both form and energy. They can hold, gain, lose, resonate with, transduce, and transmit energy. Because of this, they are different from Rupert Sheldrake's hypothesis of morphogenic fields described in *A New Science of Life*. His morphogenic fields are concerned only with form; they are neither a type of matter nor a type of energy. Sheldrake's description of the morphogenic fields and his brilliant hypothesis of formative causation describes the form aspect of SOEFs beautifully. According to Sheldrake, morphogenic fields play a causal role in the development and maintenance of the forms of systems at all levels. Sheldrake uses the term "morphic unit" as a way to describe the sub-units in a system, that is, a morphic unit for protons; another for atoms, water molecules, and muscle cells; and another for organs such as kidneys. The higher morphic fields coordinate the interplay, organization, and pattern of the smaller morphic units. Like the SOEFs, these morphogenic fields correspond to the potential state of a developing system and are present before it materializes into its final form.

Once the body is present, it becomes a focal point for the SOEFs in time and space as they emerge in their purest form. These more highly purified SOEFs resonate with the less refined SOEFs that are immersed in the biogravitational fields of the human body and thus reenergize and increase their degree of organization. This is contrary to the materialist paradigm in which the physical life form is seen as the creator of the energy fields around it. Bob Toben, in *Space, Time, and Beyond,* points out that Einstein repeatedly stresses the view in his unified field theory that *the energy field creates the form.* The emerging particle is simply a space-time concentration of the nonlinear master field (analogous to the SOEFs). To put it succinctly, these fields generate matter. The body, in this holistic paradigm, is a form stabilized by the SOEFs.

If the energy of a SOEF is dispersed, the organizing field is disrupted and the living system operates in a less organized way. This is one important aspect in which the form of SOEFs specifically differs from Sheldrake's theory of morphogenic fields. This dissipation, which drives the system toward disorganization, can be termed "entropy." In concrete terms, the dissipation of the SOEF means imperfect cell replication, poorer enzymatic function, decreased capacity for biochemical transmutation, and increased tendency toward chronic dis-ease. When the SOEFs are significantly depleted, this translates into aging.

We lose the energy of SOEFs in a variety of ways. One example is through the influence of frequencies. A frequency can maintain (if it's the perfect frequencies or subset of frequencies as often used in frequency healing), deplete, or destroy a SOEF. SOEFs are not energized by frequencies. Frequencies have been proven to deplete or destroy SOEFs. They have never been shown to create a SOEF. Only connection with the energetic continuum and the conversion of tachyon into the SOEF's perfect form can create form. As another example, the SOEFs of cooked foods are substantially depleted. In order to assimilate cooked food completely we must literally reenergize the incoming food's SOEFs directly from our own life force, depleting the energy of our SOEFs. Another example is highly refined white bread. The chromium that is necessary to aid its assimilation into the system has been depleted in the processing and must be supplied by the body. Eventually, the body becomes depleted of chromium. The SOEFs in foods are also disrupted by food-processing procedures, especially food-radiation procedures, which use up to 100,000 rads (a chest X-ray is a quarter to a half of a rad). The energetic value of the irradiated food, in terms of its ability to increase our total SOEF energy, is destroyed. When we eat high-energy, unprocessed food, the result is just the opposite; the energy of the SOEFs is enhanced.

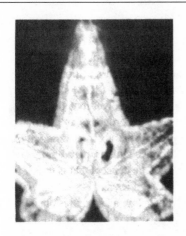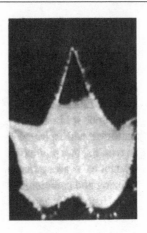

Kirlian photography demonstrates the form of SOEFs. What is critical to our understanding about these SOEFs is that they exist prior to the existence of the physical form. They are not emanated from the physical form like the magnetic field lines of a bar magnet. SOEFs are a template for physical biological forms and structures. This picture shows an energy pattern in the shape of a complete leaf surrounding a half-missing leaf. This would not happen if the field were actually emanating from the molecular structure of the physical leaf.

When SOEFs are energized, they develop a more structured and defined organization that better maintains the form and function of the human system. This energizing reverses entropy. It is this property of the SOEFs that reverses the aging process. A nice physical model for this is shown in Figure 1. Brown sugar is added to water. At first (1), it has no defined form; it lies in a disorganized pile on the bottom. When we add vortexual energy to the system by stirring with a spoon (2), the pile of brown sugar is pulled upward into a more defined form. When we stop the spoon and hold it in the water, it disrupts the vortexual pattern, the energy in the system is diminished, the brown sugar particles begin to lose their well-defined form (3), and entropy takes place. In the same way, the vortexual energy patterns of the different SOEFs create different patterns of matter as they move into the realm of time and space and begin to organize into a physical pattern. The more energy they have, the better-defined and organized are the physical structures they are manifesting. The intertwined vortex structures of RNA and DNA are archetypal physical manifestations of vortex forms. They, of course, represent the key to cellular organization. Tachyon energy only energizes the SOEFs and therefore only slows or reverses entropy and aging.

13

Figure 1

Any mental and emotional tension in the system decreases the energy coming into the system by thickening and misaligning the subtle bodies. Because the chakras are not getting the normal energy they need to function from direct external sources, they pull more from the central kundalini vortex. This too results in a blockage of the transcendence process by depleting the energy of the kundalini vortex. Tachyon energy reverses entropy and disorganization on the physical energy level, and it also energizes and organizes the SOEFs on the subtle body level and therefore can be used to reverse stress-caused entropy on the subtle body and chakra level.

Everything needed to create perfect order is contained in zero-point energy and functions with absolute perfection on that level. The fascinating order and balance in nature reveal how perfectly life functions when the creative order emerging from zero-point energy is condensed into tachyon energy, allowing the SOEFs to convert the energy into what we know as our physical world. Disharmony, dis-ease, and degeneration are not signs of the capriciousness of nature but are the results of a lifestyle that disorganizes the subtle organizing energy fields and therefore creates entropy, or aging.

Chronic and degenerative dis-eases, as well as life-threatening self-destruct..ᵥ behavioral patterns, are found only in human beings. Humans are the only life form on Earth that actually works against the rules of nature. In India, it is called *prajna pratihara,* or crimes against wisdom. Because we lack the wisdom to live healthy lifestyles, we accelerate entropy in the form of degenerative dis-eases. Only humans and domesticated animals suffer from rheumatism, diabetes, heart dis-ease, hypertension, atherosclerotic cardiovascular dis-ease, multiple sclerosis, allergies, osteoporosis, and all the other degenerative dis-eases of civilization.

CHAPTER 2

THE ENERGETIC
CONTINUUM

It is desirable to realign ourselves with our natural state of harmony and health by clearing all the blockages in the energetic continuum. By doing this we open ourselves up to the flow of the continuum from the zero-point to the tachyon into the subtle organizing energy fields in a way that energizes the energy fields and restructures them, so that we create neg-entropy or anti-aging.

The energetic continuum begins with the continual flow of energy from unlimited zero-point energy, without form and without vibration, moving faster than the speed of light. From the zero-point, energy contracts into its faster-than-light tachyon form, then to the SOEFs just prior to the speed of light. Subtle organizing energy fields create and maintain the energetic matrix from which all physical forms are made. The energetic continuum ranges from infinite formless expansion to finite contraction of form. A simple analogy can be seen in the ocean: it contains an infinite number of droplets within it, yet like zero-point energy it is formless. If you were to remove one drop from the ocean, you would still have everything the ocean has, but now it is in a form. Likewise, tachyon contains everything that exists within zero-point energy, but now it is in a form.

The graph on page 18 shows a two-dimensional rendering of the energetic continuum.

Once we understand that this continuum exists, we can understand the effect of blockages in the flow of energy down through the continuum. This is a significant insight into our theory of holistic healing. Once we realize that in illnesses

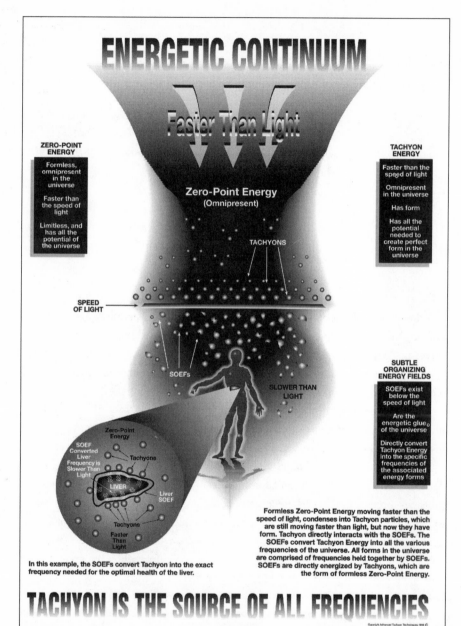

we have a blockage in the flow of the energetic continuum, it follows that this blockage is what needs to be cleared. The blockage is defined, in essence, as a disorder or chaos in the energetic continuum causing an energy deficiency. These blockages in the continuum are in the form of particular frequencies that ultimately create disorder, dis-ease, or chaos in the physical body. The tachyon energy, because it is the source of all frequencies, organizes and energizes the SOEFs, providing the potential to restore natural flow of energy through the energetic continuum. Tachyon energy creates an anti-entropy effect; it organizes that which is disorganized. Tachyon realigns and restores the SOEFs to their natural state of order and balance, thus creating health. A simple example of this would be someone who experienced an emotional stress that continued without any release or balance, causing a blockage of energy in the emotional body. This blockage in the natural flow of energy causes an energy deficiency between the emotional body and a part of the physical body. Let's say the blockage is causing a deficiency in the lower lumbar. The person may begin to experience lower back pain. If the stress continues, the situation could escalate into severe back pain, ruptured disc problems, or even degenerative disc dis-ease. Any time you have a part of the energetic continuum blocked, the organ or system that is left in a deficient energetic state will ultimately succumb to one of this world's many degenerative dis-eases—and this applies to almost all dis-eases. We are co-creators in our state of health.

Tachyon energy, when focused into the specific deficient area, reorganizes and energizes the disrupted SOEFs and therefore allows the blockage to dissipate. When the blockage is removed, the body is able to reconnect to its energetic continuum. Connection to the energetic continuum means an increased flow of energy, which is what the life force is about. There is, in essence, an increased flow of life force when a person's stress is relieved.

Tachyon energy in itself is not a frequency, yet it does contain the potential of all frequencies. This is important to understand because there is a lot of confusion about the different frequencies of energies being used. Once you understand that tachyon is the source all frequencies and enhances all frequencies, yet is not a frequency, you begin to understand the place of tachyon in the spectrum. Tachyon energy interacts with the SOEFs that absorb the portion needed to energize them, enhancing and strengthening their frequency. All frequencies, like photon or orgone or light waves, can become more coherent and balanced when tachyon is used to energize their SOEFs. This applies to everything that we know of in our existence.

BIOPHOTONS AND THE PHYSICAL BODY

The physical body is the last part in the energetic continuum of a human being. The body's metabolism is extremely complex and highly sensitive. Every disruption of metabolic processes can result in malfunctions, which can then manifest as dis-ease symptoms.

The coordination and regulation of the molecular activity in our cells is the result of signal transmissions via biophotons, or light particles. These biophotons transmit the life energy they convert from the SOEFs and therefore are the link between the tachyon-SOEF and the physical body. The light particles then supply all active molecules of our metabolism with this life energy. Certain molecules such as DNA, RNA, enzymes, chlorophyll, and helix-shaped proteins have the capacity to coordinate the metabolism via these biophotons. Such molecules are called LM (live macromolecules).

This phenomenon explains many questions that cannot be answered by a strictly biochemical examination of cellular metabolism. It serves to clarify, for example, why this incredibly complex mechanism can function with such precision. It further explains why 97 percent of DNA consists of material that does not contain the information of our hereditary makeup. This DNA material is made up of so-called introns. Introns are component parts of the DNA that emit and receive biophotons. The transmission of the introns regulates intercellular and intracellular communication. When the photon energy is diminished, the intra- and intercellular communication, which coordinates the entire cellular metabolism, diminishes and we have an increase in cellular disorganization.

On the physical level, toxic and unnatural substances, as well as a deficiency of intact LM, are the factors that inhibit the flow of life energy. A raw-food diet that is rich in enzymes and LM, and at the same time free of unnatural substances, can serve as the physical basis for a smooth and effective flow of the life energy.

JOYOUS LIFE AS A SUPERCONDUCTOR

Unfolding our spiritual potential, attaining harmony in all areas of life, and establishing radiant health are goals that are directly dependent upon how well the cosmic life energy, emanating from the unmanifested zero-point energy, can flow through the various subtle levels and into our physical body. We do not have to turn ourselves into something that we really aren't; we can, instead, become "superconductors." A superconductor is a material that has no resistance to the flow of energy. To achieve optimal health, we need to create spiritual, mental, emotional, and physical bodies that are superconductors—that have no resistance to the flow of the cosmic energy coming into our life through the energetic continuum. To the degree to which we do not create any impediments to the flow of cosmic energy going through our system, our spiritual potential unfolds and we are able to establish radiant health in our lives, and consequently high levels of joy. As superconductors we reach toward a state of optimal health and the highest level of order in the process of order/chaos/order/chaos/order. At this point we are at complete harmony, in optimal health, and in ecstatic communion with the radiant one, God. This is what happens when we begin to clear all the blocks. Each block we clear adds to the joy of the cosmic energy flowing through us. We can actually feel this. This is not necessarily a state of enlightenment, but a state of experiencing the divine energy of God. As we repeatedly experience it (and then experience the divine energy consistently filling us with joy, peace, and contentment), we begin to understand that we are that divine energy. This is a form of what we jokingly call "divine behavior modification."

We continually have choices in our life that we have to make. Do we choose to create a lifestyle, diet, and a way of being in the world that helps us become more and more a superconductor? Or do we choose to ignore the laws of nature and the divine, in essence creating more chaos, entropy, and degeneration in our lives? And how do we make these choices? Is it simply a conscious choice or are there other factors going on that influence this very critical life-enhancing or life-depleting choice that we make? What determines whether we choose to become more of a superconductor or less of a super conductor for the energetic continuum?

THE BIFURCATION POINT

In the order/chaos/order theory, the term "bifurcation point" really helps elucidate whether we move toward health or toward illness at any particular point. This happens regardless of whether we actually choose it or our bodies go that direction without our conscious awareness. By understanding the concept of bifurcation point, we'll get a much deeper insight into the human process. Ilya Prigogine, a chemist who was one of the Nobel Prize winners of 1977, coined the term. He found that the development of an organized system is not a linear process; there is a particular pattern that it follows and, at some point as the human body is confronted with stresses, its capacity for adaptation to the stresses becomes exhausted. When overwhelmed, the body cannot respond in an organized way to incoming stimuli.

21

This point of overwhelm is called the bifurcation point. It is the point or moment of truth in which the body either breaks down—allowing dis-ease-enhancing factors that have been present for many years to cause the manifestation of dis-ease—or there is a move toward better health, elevating the body to a higher level of order. This moment determines the future of a cell, organ, or the entire body-mind complex. We see this clinically all the time. People appear to be okay and then suddenly they develop, for example, severe chronic fatigue. What appears to be a sudden event isn't. What's happening is they have been building the stress all along until suddenly their body reaches overwhelm and they go over the edge into chaos. There is a point here in which the body in some way chooses to either go into more stuck chaos and the development of dis-ease, or to move into a higher level of order, creating a quantum leap that enhances the body's functioning.

In human systems, how to affect which way a system would move, either toward a higher order or toward dis-ease, was always a mystery. Today we now have a way to influence the direction a system will go. In 1990, David Wagner developed specialized tools and techniques that encourage a bifurcation of a system during a treatment administered by a trained Tachyon practitioner to help achieve this effect. The application of tachyonized materials to human systems specifically empowers us humans to successfully move through the chaos-bifurcation point into a new level of health. This has been an exciting breakthrough. For the first time, a Tachyon Practitioner can assist a client through a bifurcation point which results in a powerful shift toward youthing and healing.

Free will, however, has the power to influence the bifurcation point away from evolving into a higher level of health and order. This explains why some people, no matter what healers are seen or modalities are applied, do not heal. A simple example of the role of free will is in the animal kingdoms where animals have instinct but no free will. This explains why a dog can't consciously walk in front of a train and commit suicide, whereas a human being using free will can consciously walk in front of a train. Free will gives us the power to hold onto any physical, emotional, mental, spiritual stress or disease.

ATTUNEMENT

One of the important aspects of holistic healing is the ability to move through the bifurcation point. Our level of attunement at that moment will determine the direction our being will move: either toward order or chaos, health or dis-ease, joy or sadness, or more or less communion with the divine. Attunement, in essence, is the creation of a flow of organized energy resonating within the person such that when they reach a bifurcation point, they automatically and naturally go toward balance. This movement toward balance (otherwise referred to as the healing process) is greatly enhanced by the use of Tachyonized materials. Research has shown that when Tachyonized materials are provided to a localized area, the area continually benefits from neg-entropic effects. Whatever frequency is needed is converted into biological energy by the SOEFs so that the body may heal itself.

Here's a simple case study, from Christina Cummings, M.D. "Eight weeks ago I sprained my ankle, sustaining severe injury including swelling, ecchymosis (bruising), and pain, incapacitating me from bearing weight on that ankle. An orthopedic surgeon who examined my foot suggested I have X rays taken because of the amount of bruising present, which led him to believe I had fractured my ankle. The X rays were negative. This type of injury would ordinarily take at least two to four weeks to completely and comfortably bear weight on, let alone run on. After two days of using Tachyonized cells and a Tachyonized sports wrap, the swelling was completely gone and I was able to hop up and down on the previously injured ankle totally pain-free!"

This has been the missing part of Prigogine's explanation of why things move to a state of order or increased disorder. On a cosmic level, when we start to look at the whole energetic structure of the body, mind, spirit, and emotional complex, attunement with tachyon energy enhances our connection with the energetic continuum at the highest level. Ultimately, attunement enhances our communion with the divine. When we are attuned or aligned with tachyon energy in a particular way that makes the higher cosmic energies more accessible to us, we are more likely to make choices for healing when we reach the bifurcation point. The energy gathered through Tachyonized materials has the potential to heal not only the micro, but also to restore the body, mind, and spirit alignment of the macro system.

The tachyon energy enhances our ability to attune on all levels. Attunement covers a wide range of the relationship to the vortexual energies. We can be attuned to the point at which our body, or a particular organ or joint, can move through the bifurcation point toward health and balance. We can also attune more intensely so that we are reaching up to higher levels of the cosmic energy, experiencing in our life the grace of God.

Tachyon energy is the first evolutionary condensation of creation. Contained within it is inherently all the potential needed to feed the SOEFs and create perfect form on the planet. This condensation flows and continually condenses, ultimately condensing itself into physical form. Tachyon physics describe the link between the form and formless and offers us the possibility of opening an "exogate" (a magical doorway between form and the formless) into All That Is.

Tachyon energy possesses within itself the complete potential of all creation. Again, tachyons do not have a specific frequency, but rather are the source of all frequencies. Our body-mind complex can only access zero-point energy via tachyon, which is converted into frequencies by SOEFs. This is the key to healing. Clearing blocks in an energetic continuum enhances the healing frequency of each SOEF for each organ.

At zero-point energy there are no frequencies. Zero-point energy condenses and densifies into tachyon energy where there still are no frequencies and it is still faster than the speed of light. Just prior to the speed of light the tachyon energy interfaces with the SOEFs, through which it becomes particularized and divides itself into all measurable slower-than-light frequencies. At this point it is no longer tachyon. These frequencies include all that has been perceived. As the energy continues the densification process it begins to pass through all our subtle bodies. This densification from tachyon energy is directly responsible for all subtle and material forms.

The human body is a perfect example of an energetic continuum. We see the energy continue to densify, energizing all the SOEFs and ultimately creating multidimensional levels of form in the body-mind complex. This includes forms at the sub-zero level as well as complex cellular organ and tissue levels and the more subtle levels of emotions and mind. In order to better clarify this, we will take the simple example of a human liver. At the physical level, it exists inside of us, it is fed, and it has its own direct alignment with creation through its own energetic continuum. At the same time, it is part of the greater whole of our physical, emotional, and mental body. Both are avenues through which tachyon energy works with us. Because of this, we have the opportunity for ultimate attunement, clearing and potentially creating perfect balance in our energetic continuum. Therefore, we can say that every cell, substructure, organ structure, tissue, and bone has the potential to align and commune with All That Is. When this is happening, of course, we have perfect health. We now have a complete practical and theoretical understanding of holistic healing that includes healing and energizing the SOEFs on every level of the energetic continuum. Tachyon energy energizes and balances all levels including the spiritual, mental, emotional, and physical.

The tachyon flow energizes the SOEFs, bringing coherency to their fields and therefore health to the body. In modern physics, we can say it creates neg-entropy, which is the concept of bringing order out of disorder. Tachyon energy actually creates "youthing." Aging, or entropy, involves the dissolution of the field so it loses its coherency and therefore its ability to function. Aging occurs when the RNA and DNA don't divide in a way that is orderly or systematic. When this happens, the cell functions are not as well defined, the tissues and organs don't work as well, and the body is not as healthy. On the other hand, youthing is the result of neg-entropy in which each field becomes orderly. When RNA and DNA divide in an orderly way, the cells function in an orderly way. That means the organs and tissues function in an orderly way, and then of course the body functions in an orderly way. An extreme form of entropy is cancer.

CHAPTER 3

MEASURING THE BIOLOGICAL EFFECT OF TACHYONIZED MATERIALS

Tachyonized material energizes and structures the SOEF, and therefore creates an anti-aging effect. For this chapter we will show you a variety of research which scientifically and visually makes this point.

MEASURING THE SOEFS WITH KIRLIAN PHOTOGRAPHY

Kirlian photography is one method for measuring the effects of SOEF strength. One study, discussed below, incorporated ripe fruit. Once the fruit is removed from the mother plant, a natural phenomenon occurs in which the SOEFs begin to break down and decrease in strength. Because the source energy from the mother plant no longer supports the SOEFs, we see a continual breakdown of the energy fields until the fruit finally decays. This breakdown is easy to see pictorially using Kirlian photography.

In the following study of fruits and vegetables, all measurements were taken with the Corona Discharge Imagine Research Model KP 40. The results were 100 percent consistent with every subject tested. Two typical examples are a peach and a plum. Once photographed, the fruits were immediately moved into a space containing a Tachyonized silica disc. After twenty minutes of charging the SOEFs with a focused Tachyonized disk, the peach and the plum were re-photographed. The tachyon field was focused through these Tachyonized silica disks, and was converted by the SOEFs of the peach and plum into the exact frequencies needed. This significantly increased the biological energy of the fruit and produced a dramatic neg-entropic effect on the biological systems. ("Neg-entropy" is a term used in modern physics to explain the concept of bringing order out of disorder.) These

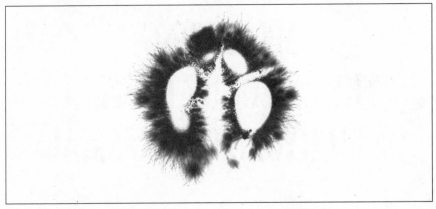

This KIRLIAN photo is of a non-organic peach.
The energetic value of the peach once removed from the tree will continually decrease.
This is the natural aging process as the subtle organizing energy fields begin to break down,
and the peach begins to move into a higher state of disorder and chaos as it rots.

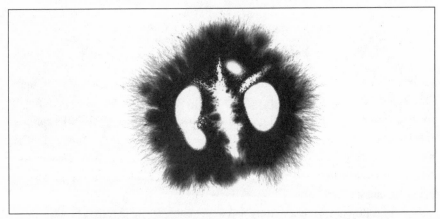

This KIRLIAN photo is of the same ripe non-organic peach.
The difference between the two peach photos is 20 minutes inside a Tachyon field created
by a Tachyonized Silica Disc antenna. The subtle organizing energy field and therefore the
entire energy field of the peach is greatly enhanced.

tests clearly demonstrate that the subtle organizing energy fields of the fruit are greatly strengthened and enhanced when charged with a Tachyonized disk. It is as if the fruit were still connected to the source plant, receiving all of its energies through its natural connection with the earth, the sun, and All That Is. The fruit with the highest SOEF energy would obviously provide the body with a much higher quantity and quality of peach or plum energy when eaten.

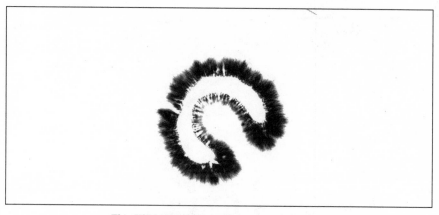

This KIRLIAN photo is of a non-organic plum.
The energetic value of the plum once removed from the tree will continually decrease.
This is the natural aging process as the subtle organizing energy fields begin to break down,
and the plum moves into a higher state of disorder and chaos as it rots.

This KIRLIAN photo is of the same ripe non-organic plum.
The difference between the two plum photos is 20 minutes inside a Tachyon field created
by a Tachyonized Silica Disc antenna. The subtle organizing energy field and therefore the
entire energy field of the plum is greatly enhanced.

The following Kirlian photo study demonstrates that plants in potted soil display significant increases in their overall energetic field after receiving a tachyon treatment. Out of all the live plants tested and photographed, this burgundy ficus represents the average effect observed. Photographic research has found that plants connected to the soil require much less time to increase the SOEFs than harvested plants or fruits. In the case of this ficus, only ten minutes elapsed

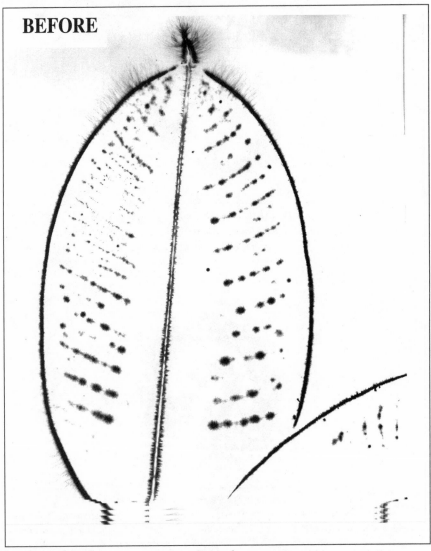

BEFORE

Figure 2.
This Kirlian photo was taken while the leaf was attached to the potted plant.

between the two photos. The differences between Figure 2 and Figure 3 are due to the fact that a Tachyonized Silica Disk was taped on the bottom of the pot of the plant in Figure 3.

These photos again and again demonstrate that Tachyon alone enhances the SOEFs of all living organisms, including humans.

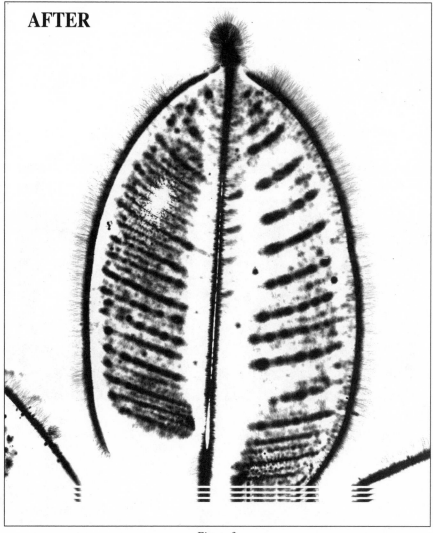

Figure 3.
This Kirlian photo was taken while the leaf was attached to the potted plant. A Tachyonized Silica Disk was taped to the bottom of the pot, so the plant's SOEF is stronger.

TACHYONIZED SAND INCREASES SOEFs AND STIMULATES GROWTH.
This study monitored the growth of four Pampas Grass plants of the Cortaderia Selloana variety. One plant had Tachyonized Sand, which is a silica-based material, worked into the soil around the root ball. The increase in growth was extremely dramatic, as the vitality and strength of this plant far exceeded that of the other three. This test demonstrated that Tachyon energy energizes all the Subtle Organizing Energy Fields, stimulating the entire energy of the plant, which flourished beyond all expectations.

This pampas grass is relatively small compared to the treated grass. It is growing nicely without any difficulties, yet it is still considerably smaller than the Tachyon energy-treated plant. This plant did not have any special Tachyon treatments.

This pampas grass is also small. This plant did not have any special Tachyon treatments

This pampas grass is closest to the treated grass, and therefore we believe through its natural connection with the treated grass it grew larger than the grass farther away. Measuring this one, it is about half the size of the treated plant. This plant did not have any special Tachyon energy treatments.

One growing season before these photos were taken this pampas grass had special Tachyonized sand worked into the soil. As you can see by this photo this particular plant is about three times larger than the plants to the far left. When this test started all four pampas grass were the same size. In fact, this particular one was slightly smaller, and for this reason it was selected for this test. This is the only plant that had Tachyonized materials mixed into the sand.

*Tom before enjoying a Tachyon
Energy source.*

*Tom's photo shows an increase in
his measured energy field, 20 minutes after taking Tachyonized water
and wearing a Tachyon pendant.*

*Robert prior to enjoying
Tachyon Energy.*

*Robert, 20 minutes after taking
Tachyonized water and wearing a
Tachyon pendant.*

HUMAN ENERGY PHOTOS

These photos were taken with a special "aura camera." We have included them in this book to show yet another example of how the energy field of a biological system increases when the SOEFs are energized using Tachyon Energy. These photos clearly demonstrate the energizing effects of Tachyon. As Tachyon energizes the SOEFs, the SOEFs convert the energy into all the frequencies of the body, balancing the natural frequencies of the user. In these "aura photos" we can clearly see that the photo taken after using a Tachyonized energy antenna for 20 minutes shows a dramatic increase in balance and expansion in the energetic bodies.

The photos on these two pages are part of an extensive research study done at the House of Well-Being in Engetried, Germany. The researchers, Herta and Dr. Hansen, objectively wanted to identify the effects of Tachyonized materials on the human energetic system. As can be seen in Figure 5, the energetic outline of the hands is weak and in many areas the energy isn't even measurable. These energy deficiency areas of the hands and fingers specifically represent energy deficiencies in the body.

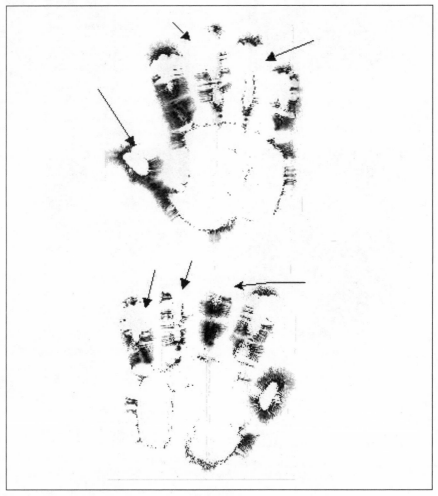

Figure 5
*This Kirlian photo shows many energy deficiencies, which are interpreted by the lack of
"solidity," or holes in the subtle organizing energy fields.*

After each client was measured, Dr. Hansen then administered 10 drops of Tachyonized water sublingually and had the client wear a Tachyonized pendant for a total of 15 minutes. Dr. Hansen then remeasured each client. New measurements captured and made obvious the neg-entropic effects of Tachyon. The meridians were energetically reconnected suggesting energetic balance on the physical level.

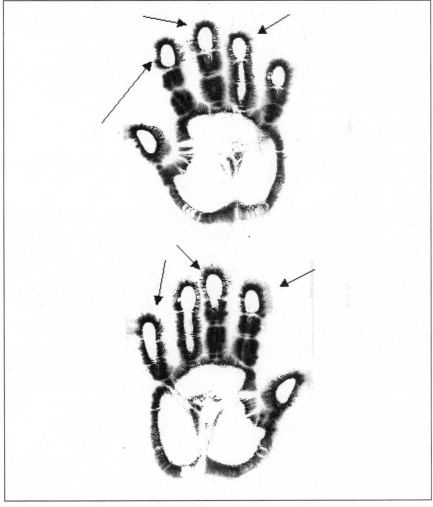

Figure 6
In this Kirlian photo the client was treated to 10 drops of Tachyonized water and wore a Tachyon Pendant for 15 minutes. Notice how the Tachyon has energetically reconnected all the meridians.

Ma Prem Jwala, at the Osho Multiversity in Pune, India, conducted similar research. Ma Prem Jwala's extensive study measured the meridian systems using advanced Kirlian diagnostic techniques invented by Dr. Peter Mandell. Using Dr. Mandell's diagnostic techniques, Ma Prem Jwala was able to diagnose many of the energetic deficiencies in the body.

The research illuminated the neg-entropic effects which bring balance first to the energetic body and then to the physical body. This creates a real opportunity for permanent healing. Her research concurred with Dr. Hansen's as she demonstrated the effectiveness of Tachyonized materials as healing tools.

These insights were instrumental to the Multiversity's open invitation to David Wagner to teach advanced methods of applying Tachyonized materials to health care professionals there. He has been teaching in Pune annually since 1996.

TACHYONIZED MATERIALS AND PLANTS

The prototype of the following study was done in 1992. It has been duplicated countless times in this form and with the use of many varieties of plants, including both cut and potted. In the photos on page 37 are two rosebuds cut from the same vine. Rosebud A was placed into regular distilled water, and rosebud B was placed into pure Tachyonized water. Rosebud A opened, the stem collapsed, and the flower wilted after several days. This represents the normal life expectancy of this variety of rose. The water for rosebud A was then replaced with pure Tachyonized water. The stem became erect and rosebud A reopened for another three days. Rosebud B, which had been sitting in the Tachyonized water all along, stayed open for nine days without any signs of wilting. We conclude from this that the Tachyonized water continually energized Rosebud B's SOEFs. The SOEFs converted the tachyon energy into the exact frequency needed for rosebud B to stay balanced and alive. From this we can postulate that Tachyonized materials seem to slow the effects of the aging (positive entropy) process. In the case of rosebud A, the effect seemed to be a partial reversal of the aging process. With rosebud B, where Tachyonized materials were used from the beginning, we see an extension of the life process, as the stem grew roots and was planted. Subsequently the stem developed into a beautiful rose bush. Tachyonized materials have the ability to keep a biological system in balance by promoting the vitality and health of the system.

Rose A *is suffering from the aging process. It has been severed from the vine and placed in purified water, yet it continues to slowly die.*

Rose B *is experiencing the effects of Tachyon. The flower is absorbing Tachyon energy converted by the SOEFs into the exact frequency needed to sustain a balanced life. It is as if the flower defies the aging process.*

Rose B

Rose A

WHAT IS TACHYON ENERGY?

Basically, tachyon consists of subatomic particles whose velocity always exceeds the speed of light. Their existence appears to be consistent with the theory of relativity. The theory of relativity is traditionally thought to apply only to particles traveling at less than the speed of light. This may change since the existence of tachyon has been demonstrated mathematically and its effects have been measured. Ordinary particles only exist at less than the speed of light. Tachyon only exists at speeds that surpass that of light. Although it's difficult for twentieth-century people to conceive of such energy, Dr. Callahan proved the existence of tachyon using fig leaves and an oscilloscope. He also demonstrated its faster-than-light velocity. Presently, Advanced Tachyon Technologies, a U.S. corporation, provides Tachyonized materials which act as antennas that harness the power of tachyon energy.

EXPERIMENTS TO PROVE
TACHYON ENERGY'S PRACTICAL USE

The purpose of this research is to discover if the theoretical energy focalized by the Tachyonized materials manufactured by Advanced Tachyon Technologies can be used as actual healing tools that support the life force. The following set of experiments was documented by Pacifica Goddard in San Rafael, California, in February 1994.

Materials:

Purified water	Tachyonized water
12 carnations	18 sunflower seeds
24 violas	Two 8mm Tachyonized Energy Cells
Two 13mm Tachyonized Energy Cells	2 bowls
2 paper towels	2 identical vases
Notepad	

Hypothesis:

Tachyon energy will be proven genuine. I recently sprained my ankle, so I took the opportunity to test a Tachyonized product, an ankle wrap. I immediately felt warmth and the pain began to subside. Within twenty-four hours my ankle was bearing normal weight and I was able to walk up and down my stairs. A strain of this magnitude would have normally taken at least a week to bear full body weight. Due to this experience I felt further testing was warranted. Was the healing of my ankle coincidence or real life-force energy at work? If tachyon energy is real, I want to explore the extent of its effects; therefore I have devised a number of experiments. Particularly interesting is Experiment 4 (page 45), a severe situation in which water-deprived plants are studied. Throughout these experiments, I make the following comparisons:

- Between Tachyonized items and regular items
- Between Tachyonized Energy Cells and Tachyonized water
  (One main difference I noticed was that the plants exposed to the Tachyonized Energy Cells were slightly thicker, fluffier, and bushier, and frequently tended to be just slightly lengthier.)
- Between a 13mm and an 8mm Tachyonized Energy Cell
  (I was not able to detect any differences the size of the cells may have had on the growth of the plant.)

Procedures, Journal Data, and Experiment Results

I had five different experiments running. The procedures used varied, so in order to clarify the exact methodology, I will list each procedure and experiment separately.

Eighteen sunflower seeds are tested. Nine are germinated in Tachyonized water and nine are germinated in purified water for the control.

NOTE ONE: All the Tachyonized items are on Windowsill One. All the regularly watered items are on Windowsill Two. The windowsills are always at the same precise temperature and each item gets the same amount of sunshine.

NOTE TWO: I often mention that I did something such as "watered all the plants" on either windowsill. When I say "all the plants," I am referring exclusively to all of the plants in that particular experiment.

I began with 2 bowls, 2 paper towels folded in quarters, 18 sunflower seeds, a one-cup measuring cup, 1 teaspoon purified water, and 1 teaspoon Tachyonized water. I lined the bowls with the paper towels and filled each of them with a half cup of water. I placed 9 sunflower seeds in each bowl and then added 1 teaspoon of purified water to one of the bowls. I added 1 teaspoon of Tachyonized water to the other bowl. Every other day I added various amounts of purified water to each bowl (always measured precisely so no bowl would be left with less water than the other) and recorded the progress.

Experiment 1

January 19:

The 18-sunflower-seeds test begins. Nine are germinated in Tachyonized water and nine are germinated in purified water for the control.

January 23:

I give the bowl on Windowsill One 1 tablespoon of purified water and 1 teaspoon of Tachyonized water. I give the bowl on Windowsill Two $1^{1}/_{3}$ tablespoons of purified water.

Tachyonized seeds (Windowsill One): Eight of the sunflower seeds have shells that are cracked. Four of these have small roots sticking out, which range from 2mm long to 5mm long.

Regular seeds (watered with purified water on Windowsill Two): Seven seeds have shells that are cracked at the top. No roots have emerged at this point.

January 26:

Five and $^{1}/_{3}$ tablespoons of purified water are given to the bowl on Windowsill Two; 5 tablespoons of purified water and 1 teaspoon of Tachyonized water are given to the bowl on Windowsill One.

Tachyonized seeds (Windowsill One): Every one of the seeds has a crack in its shell and each one has a white root coming out of it. The lengths of the roots range from 2mm to 11mm.

Regular seeds watered with purified water on Windowsill Two: Eight of these sunflower seeds have cracked.

January 28:

Six and $^{1}/_{3}$ tablespoons of purified water are added to the bowl on Windowsill Two. Six tablespoons of purified water and 1 teaspoon of Tachyonized water are added to the bowl on Windowsill One.

Tachyonized seeds (Windowsill One): The length of the roots spans 3mm to 14mm. Only one of these roots has a slightly browned tip, which was less than a millimeter long.

Regular seeds (watered with purified water on Windowsill Two): One of the seeds is still just cracked but a root is about to emerge. The root lengths range from 4mm to 14mm long (discounting the just-visible root, which has not emerged). Four of these roots have browned tips; three of the browned tips are 4 to 5mm long and one is 2mm long. The brown tips indicate a significant decay of the roots.

January 30:

Three and one-half tablespoons of purified water are added to the bowl on

Windowsill Two. Three tablespoons of purified water and 1 teaspoon of Tachyonized water are added to the bowl on Windowsill One.

Tachyonized seeds: The nine roots range from 11mm to 34mm. One root has a browned tip 1$^1/_2$mm long.

Regular seeds: The one seed that had barely cracked on January 29 has a root that is visible but not out of the shell yet. The length of the other roots ranges from 9mm to 30mm. Five of the roots have browned tips. One is a full centimeter long, two are 6mm long, one is 2mm long, and one is less than a millimeter long.

January 31:

Three and $^1/_3$ tablespoons of purified water are added to the bowl on Windowsill Two. Three tablespoons of purified water and 1 teaspoon of Tachyonized water are added to the bowl on Windowsill One.

February 2:

Nine and $^1/_3$ tablespoons of purified water are added to the bowl on Windowsill Two. Nine tablespoons of purified water and 1 teaspoon of Tachyonized water are added to the bowl on Windowsill One.

Tachyonized seeds: These seeds are still doing great! Their roots are still exceptionally stiff when pressed. One of the seeds has come entirely out of its shell and its leaves are spreading and growing. Two others are more than halfway out of their shells. The root lengths range from 15mm to 38mm. Four of these roots have browned tips. One browned tip is 3mm long while two are 2mm and another is 6mm. The other roots do not have brown tips nor do they show any signs of decay.

Regular seeds: Some of the roots on these seeds have actually shrunk! It seems that such extensive time in the water has made them start to decay; some parts of the ends of the roots have fallen off. The range of length is now 7mm to 26$^1/_2$mm. Every one of these roots has a browned tip except for the one root that is just starting to emanate from its small shell with a fresh white stub. One root has a browned end 20mm long. Three of the roots have brown ends, one 11mm long, another 12mm, and the last 2mm long. The decaying state of these roots is easy to see. The differences between these two experiments are undeniable.

February 6:

The results that I observed during the past few weeks are truly remarkable. I can now safely say that the Tachyonized seeds sprouted and grew more quickly than the regular seeds. The Tachyonized materials seemed to supply the seeds with enough life-force energy that they appeared to defy death and decay. They substantially outlived the ones in the other experiment and continued to grow while the other seeds decayed.

I conclude that Tachyonized water helped the seeds sprout faster, grow lengthier roots, and stay healthy and alive much longer.

Experiment 2

Eight violas are tested. Four are grown with Tachyonized Beads beneath them and four are grown without Tachyonized Beads for the control.

I purchased two pearl-hued Tachyonized Beads (Energy Cells) and two emerald-hued Tachyonized Beads (Energy Cells). The emerald beads were the larger of the two (13mm versus 8mm). I also purchased eight young potted violas of the same size, and a bottle of purified water. I separated and labeled four of the violas that would act as my control group. In the next two potted violas I placed one tiny Tachyonized Bead directly into the soil of each pot. The last two potted violas received small emerald Tachyonized cells buried in the soil. I watered each one with $3^1/_3$ tablespoons of water. Every other day I watered each plant with $3^1/_3$ tablespoons of purified water and recorded results.

January 19:

The eight-violas test begins.

January 23:

I water each plant with $3^1/_3$ tablespoons of purified water. No changes recorded at this time.

January 26:

Each of the eight violas is watered with $3^1/_3$ tablespoons of purified water.

Tachyonized violas (Windowsill One): While the other plants are doing extremely well, these plants are somewhat stiffer and straighter without any signs of wilting. There are several reddish leaves on them but all in all these plants are almost completely green. The plants watered with the Tachyonized charged water are much sturdier and far greener than the other plants. There are 3.5 decayed leaves per plant on average.

Regular violas (on Windowsill Two): These plants are doing well. There are several wilted red-and-brown leaves but that is to be expected. These plants aren't growing as straight as the violas with the Tachyonized beads in their soil. There are 6.25 decayed leaves per plant on average.

January 28:

Each of the eight violas is watered with $3^1/_3$ tablespoons of purified water.

January 30:

Each of the eight violas is watered with $3^1/_3$ tablespoons of purified water.

Tachyonized violas: Every plant is growing in a large mass that reaches 11cm high on average. No new decayed leaves have formed.

Regular violas: The height of the flowers is 11cm on average. The height of the rest of the foliage is $5^1/_2$cm on average. There is an average of 2.25 new decayed leaves per plant.

January 31:

Each of the eight violas is watered with $3^1/_3$ tablespoons of purified water.

February 2:

Each of the eight violas is watered with $3^1/_3$ tablespoons of purified water.

Tachyonized violas: The average height of the mass amount of foliage and flowers is $12^1/_2$cm. The average of new decayed leaves is .25 per plant.

Regular violas: The uneven growth is continuing. The flowers have sprung to a height of 12cm. The rest of the foliage is at an average height of 7cm. The leaves on these plants are of a lighter shade than those of the Tachyonized plants.

February 6:

The results that have been compiled in this experiment suggest that the Tachyonized Energy Cells helped the plants grow more quickly and healthily, with less decay. I conclude that Tachyonized Energy Cells improve the rate and evenness of growth as well as the thickness of foliage.

Experiment 3

Eight violas are tested. Four are watered with Tachyonized water and four are watered with purified water for the control.

I purchased eight violas, purified water, and a two-ounce bottle of Tachyonized water. I watered four of the violas with $3^1/_3$ tablespoons of purified water each. The other four each received 3 tablespoons of purified water and 1 teaspoon of Tachyonized water. Every other day I watered them with the same amounts.

January 19:

The experiment begins.

January 23:

Each of the plants on Windowsill One is watered with 3 tablespoons of purified water and 1 teaspoon of Tachyonized water. Each of the plants on Windowsill Two is watered with $3^1/_3$ tablespoons of purified water. No changes recorded.

January 26:

Each plant on Windowsill One is watered with 3 tablespoons of purified water and 1 teaspoon of Tachyonized water. Each plant on Windowsill Two is watered with 3^1/$_3$ tablespoons of purified water.

Tachyonized violas: Definitely more noticeable growth is observed with these plants. The plants are growing in big bushy clumps, and all are growing at almost the same rate. The plants are shorter but appear stronger and bushier. The average amount of decayed leaves is 5 per plant. The highest areas are about 8cm high on average.

Regular violas: There seems to be more uneven growth on these plants. All the flowers seem to tower above the rest of the foliage at a whopping height average of 10cm. The rest of the foliage is at an extremely low height of 4cm on average. The average amount of decayed leaves is 6.5 per plant.

NOTE: All the decayed leaves on the Tachyonized plants are near or on the bottom, which indicates that no new leaves have decayed recently. The decayed leaves on the regular plants are spread throughout the plant, which indicates that there is a continuous decaying of leaves.

January 28:

Each plant on Windowsill One is watered with 3 tablespoons of purified water and 1 teaspoon of Tachyonized water. Each plant on Windowsill Two is watered with 3^1/$_3$ tablespoons of purified water.

January 30:

Each plant on Windowsill One is watered with 3 tablespoons of purified water and 1 teaspoon of Tachyonized water. Each plant on Windowsill Two is watered with 3^1/$_3$ tablespoons of purified water.

Tachyonized violas: Average height is 10^1/$_2$cm.

Regular violas: The flowers are 11cm tall on average. The rest of the foliage averages 6cm in height.

January 31:

Each plant on Windowsill One is watered with 3 tablespoons of purified water and 1 teaspoon of Tachyonized water. Each plant on Windowsill Two is watered with 3^1/$_3$ tablespoons of purified water.

February 2:

Each plant on Windowsill One is watered with 3 tablespoons of purified water and 1 teaspoon of Tachyonized water. Each plant on Windowsill Two is watered with 3^1/$_3$ tablespoons of purified water.

Tachyonized violas: The average height of all foliage is 12cm.

Regular violas: The average height of the flowers is 12cm. The average height of the rest of the foliage is 7cm.

February 6:

The collected results imply that the Tachyonized water helped nurture the plants by making them stronger and healthier. The water helped the violas grow more quickly and more evenly than usually possible. The results in this experiment were similar to those in Experiment 2, although not as dramatic.

Experiment 4

I purchased eight violas and stopped all watering for nine days. Then I watered four of them every other day with $3^1/_3$ tablespoons of purified water each. I watered the second group of four with three tablespoons of purified water and 1 teaspoon of Tachyonized water. I continued watering every other day and recorded the results of their recovery.

January 19:

The experiment begins.

January 26:

All of the plants are still dehydrating. They are all becoming very bent and limp as they start to die.

January 28:

All the plants are extremely flaccid, feeble, and shriveled. Nothing is above 4cm in height. So now the real test begins—the four plants on Windowsill One are watered with 3 tablespoons of purified water and 1 teaspoon of Tachyonized water. The four plants on Windowsill Two are watered with $3^1/_3$ tablespoons of purified water.

Tachyonized plants are starting at the following heights: Plant One, 2cm; Plant Two, 3cm; Plant Three, 3cm; Plant Four, $3^1/_2$cm.

Regular plants are starting at the following heights: Plant One, 3cm; Plant Two, 4cm; Plant Three, 2 cm; Plant Four, $1^1/_2$cm.

January 30:

Each plant on Windowsill One is watered with 3 tablespoons of purified water and 1 teaspoon of Tachyonized water. Each plant on Windowsill Two is watered with $3^1/_3$ tablespoons of purified water.

Tachyonized violas: Plant One, $3^1/_2$cm tall; Plant Two, 5cm tall; Plant Three, 6cm tall; Plant Four, 4cm tall.

Regular violas: Plant One, 4cm tall; Plant Two, 4½cm tall; Plant Three, 2½cm tall; Plant Four, 2½cm tall.

January 31:

Each plant on Windowsill One is watered with 3 tablespoons of purified water and 1 teaspoon of Tachyonized water. Each plant on Windowsill Two is watered with 3⅓ tablespoons of purified water.

Tachyonized violas: Plant One, 5cm; Plant Two, 6cm; Plant Three, 7cm; and Plant Four, 7cm.

Regular violas: Plant One, 4½cm; Plant Two, 5cm; Plant Three, 4½cm; Plant Four, 3cm.

February 2:

Each plant on Windowsill One is watered with 3 tablespoons of purified water and 1 teaspoon of Tachyonized water. Each plant on Windowsill Two is watered with 3⅓ tablespoons of purified water.

Tachyonized violas: Plant One, 7½cm; Plant Two, 8½cm; Plant Three, 8cm; Plant Four, 10cm.

Regular violas: Plant One, 6cm; Plant Two, 7cm; Plant Three, 5½cm; Plant Four, 4cm.

February 6:

The results prove that Tachyonized energy does exist and can help heal and nurture more quickly and efficiently than generally possible. This experiment established that Tachyonized water has a rejuvenating effect on sickly plants; the energy helped the plants recover much faster than those watered with purified water alone.

Experiment 5

Twelve carnations are tested. Six are placed in a vase with Tachyonized water and sprayed with Tachyonized water, and four are placed in a vase with purified water and sprayed with purified water for the control.

I purchased six stems of carnations (each one had two flowers), purified water, Tachyonized water, and two identical vases. I put three stems (six flowers) in each vase along with seven cups of water. I added 1 tablespoon of purified water to one vase and 1 tablespoon of Tachyonized water to the other vase. I recorded the decaying process.

January 31:

The experiment begins.

February 2:

One teaspoon of Tachyonized water is added to the vase on Windowsill One. One teaspoon of purified water is added to the vase on Windowsill Two. Both vases of flowers are blooming exquisitely. No differences visible yet.

February 6:

The past few days all the flowers have flourished and bloomed most spectacularly with their dazzlingly pure white petals. Today some changes are noted in the regular flowers. Four out of the six flowers have several brown-rimmed petals. No changes are found at all in the Tachyonized carnations except for one lone brown-bordered petal among many immaculate others.

There is a huge difference between the two sets of flowers, verifying Tachyonized materials' effect on longevity. This experiment proves that a bit of Tachyonized water can keep flowers fresh longer than purified water can.

My conclusion is that somehow Advanced Tachyon Technologies has been successful in creating an energy-focusing device that in fact has rejuvenating and life-extending properties. The most significant successes are in Experiment 4. Major differences were seen between the Tachyonized plants and the regular plants. The Tachyonized plants grew stronger and stayed healthier and lived longer. What my research has proven is that this energy has a neg-entropic effect on plants—an effect that neutralizes what we would normally expect as the aging and dying process.

As all this research indicates, tachyon energy specifically energizes the SOEFs, which provides the basis of a model for all levels of healing. On the emotional and mental levels, when the emotional body is disordered, increasing Tachyonized materials energy attunement helps to bring an emotional coherency, and when the emotions come into order they have a direct effect on the next layer of the energetic continuum. In the same way, when we have mental confusion, we have a disconnection and the mind is scattered. Increasing Tachyonized materials energy attunement helps brings coherency to the functioning of the mind by reorganizing and structuring the SOEFs of the mind. Read on to learn more about Tachyon and the brain.

BRAIN RESEARCH

Mr. G. Haffelder runs the Institute for Communication and Brain Research in Stuttgart, Germany. As an independent researcher working in the area of mind mapping and left-right brain balancing for the past 20 years, he is an authority on behavioral development and works with children as well as adults in the education and development of whole brain balancing.

The following three paragraphs are a synopsis of Mr. Haffelder's research as given by him in an interview.

Three-dimensional, electro-frequency analysis of both the right- and left-brain hemispheres provides insights into the functioning and balance of the brain. Mr. Haffelder did the study at the Institute for Communication and Brain Research in Stuttgart, Germany. The client whose test data is pictured on page 49 was tested while lying down with five Tachyonized Silica Disks on the body: one disk on the top of the head or seventh chakra and one disk on each of the four lower chakras. All the disks were arranged so that the energy flowed into the body. The client was placed under mental stress by being asked a series of very difficult questions. The analytical questions included mathematics exercises that had to be verbally resolved.

The test results demonstrate the powerful ability of Tachyonized materials to balance both the right- and left-brain hemispheres. Normally this type of balance is only achieved through sustained meditation, which could include alternate nostril breathing. The analysis addressed the beta (16–30 Hz), alpha (8–12 Hz), theta (4–8 Hz), and delta (0–3 Hz) brainwaves.

Mr. Haffelder was quite fascinated by these results. Normally the stress battery of questions forces the brain into working in the beta frequencies. The test results showed an extremely balanced right- and left-brain synchronicity. Mr. Haffelder, a leader in the field, has been doing research for twenty years, in which time he has never seen a brain stay balanced during this battery of stressful and difficult technical questioning. Mr. Haffelder points out that the activity is not in the expected beta frequencies, but rather is in the theta frequencies. This means the answers to the questions were not coming directly from the brain's normal function. Mr. Haffelder notes that no matter how stressful the questions became, the brain never moved out of balance. The implications are exciting. Mr. Haffelder was so moved by the results that he incorporated Tachyonized materials into his seminars, in which he teaches children how to focus and stay balanced in difficult and stressful situations.

Mr. Haffelder's EEG studies

The following simple graphs dramatically demonstrate the beneficial effects that Tachyonized materials had on the brain. Whole-brain thinking has been proven to be highly beneficial in all aspects of life. Students, athletes, computer operators, artists, or anyone requiring increased concentration could benefit from using Tachyonized tools. The illustration on this page demonstrates the balance of right- and left-brain hemispheres to be gained by using Tachyonized disks.

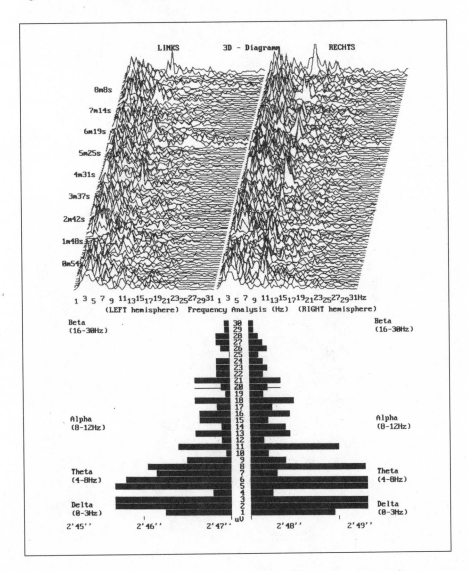

49

Brain Research with Tachyonized
Materials using EEG

Jack Stucki, RMT, CBT of the Merkaba Co., writes the following report:

Neuroscience is on the threshold of documenting a previously hidden world of unseen energies that will aid in the diagnosis and healing of injury and illness, as well as allow researchers to gain new insights into the frontiers of consciousness. Expanded human awareness may be the most important tool for exploring the holographic universe and the multidimensional human being. Research shows that specialized states of coherent consciousness display properties that go beyond ordinary "incoherent random thought" waking consciousness. By achieving highly focused levels of awareness, we are able to tap into normally unconscious and latent human abilities. We seek to document, through physio-monitoring technology, these specialized states of consciousness in an effort to access the hierarchical levels of potential enfolded within the structure of matter/energy fields and space itself.

With the intention of documenting these specialized, highly focused states of consciousness, two volunteers were selected, one male (E.F.) and one female (J.L.). Both are over thirty years old, with experiences of achieving self-imposed "theta states" through focused awareness techniques.

Both volunteers were prepped in the following manner:

- instructed that their brainwave activity would be monitored on a Lexicor QEEG computer
- told that they would be monitored during three different states of consciousness

   1) A baseline in an eyes-closed, relaxed state (Epochs 1-50); 2) In their self-imposed "theta state" (Epochs 51-150); 3) Post-state, eyes closed, relaxed (Epochs 151-312) *Tachyonized lens was then passed over various sites, without their awareness.

In an effort to maintain the integrity of the data, neither volunteer was made aware of the true purpose of the study prior to the collection of the data. My intention was not only to document these different states of consciousness, but more importantly to determine what effect, if any, the passing of a Tachyonized lens over specific electrode receptor sites would have on the data collected.

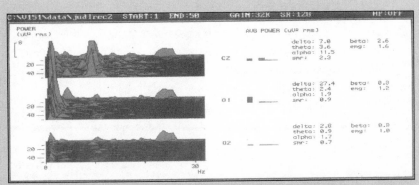

This first reading is used as the baseline. The eyes are closed and the volunteer relaxes.

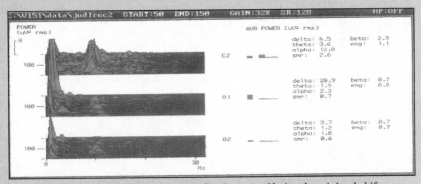

Volunteer is now in the "theta" meditative state. Notice the minimal shifts.

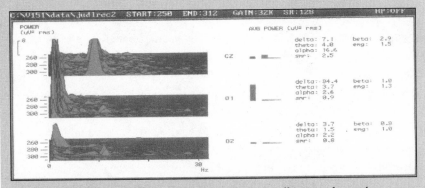

While the volunteer is in the meditative state a Tachyon cell is passed over the receptor (without their awareness) and the increase is measured. There is a profound increase in activity in the delta area of O1.

Our female volunteer, J.L., after the standard application of the cap, was monitored for a baseline and then asked to go to her "state." During that time, a number of epochs ("pages" in the data collection) were collected. A Tachyonized silica lens was then passed over the receptor sites and further epochs were recorded. Then the post-state was also documented.

In the evaluation of the data that was collected, certain key points were identified. As in any study, further research and documentation is warranted to decrease the variables and quantify the results.

I was looking for shifts in the magnitude of power, and for synchronization between the two hemispheres. Data was analyzed using only three of the sites, one at the top of the head (CZ) and two at the base of the skull (01 and 02).

Look at exhibit "1 and 2" and notice the minimal shift in power as the client goes into her relaxed state. After passing of the Tachyonized lens over the area, there was an increase in alpha activity at the crown, and the marked increase in delta activity at 01. (Exhibit "3")

Compare the data in exhibit "1" (the baseline) and exhibit "7" (with and post-Tachyonization), particularly in the alpha activity at the crown (CZ) and the delta activity at (01). Exhibit "7" averages the power over a series of epochs and these include just prior to the introduction of the Tachyonized lens and after.

This study demonstrated the superlative effect Tachyonized silica lenses have on the brain. The SOEFs convert Tachyonized materials into usable biological energy, which has the potential to awaken or even reactivate dormant portions of the brain, elevating our potential. Many stroke- and head-injury clients have reported substantial benefits in the healing and balancing of the brain function. The reason for this is that as the local SOEFs become charged and convert Tachyonized materials into the needed frequencies, they can begin a chain reaction, which has the potential to clear the associated energetic continuum, restoring balance and function.

The understanding of the energetic continuum also explains how we move from etheric energy into physical energy. Tachyonized materials don't just link the subtle organizing energy fields; it is the bridge between the different energetic worlds as it maintains the energetic continuum. For example, in the etheric realm it works with the positrons to bridge the information coming from the etheric into the physical.

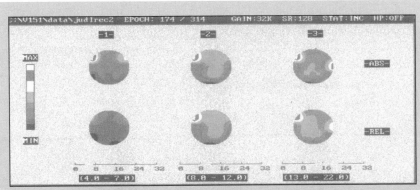

This topography is of a volunteer during relaxation. Notice the limited light areas in the topography, which represent brain activity.

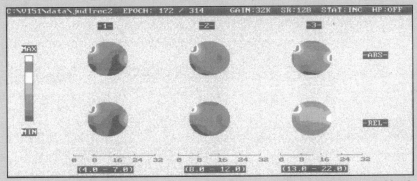

The volunteer is meditating. We see an increase in brainwave activity, represented by the lighter areas, but there is no balance between the left and right brain hemispheres.

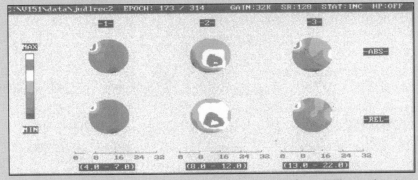

Tachyon is passed over the brain and then the results are measured. The synchronization of brainwave activity (light areas) between the hemispheres in both the alpha and beta ranges is significant! Note the balance between left and right. Tachyon increased both function and balance.

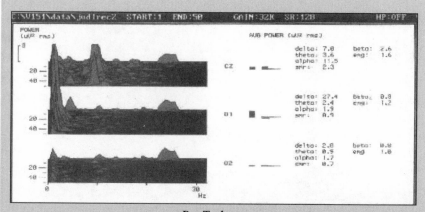

Pre-Tachyon

Test results of CZ and 01 between pre-Tachyon and post-Tachyon demonstrate the significant increase of brain activity, especially in the alpha and delta in the crown and 01. Remember that the volunteer was never aware of what we were testing, nor when.

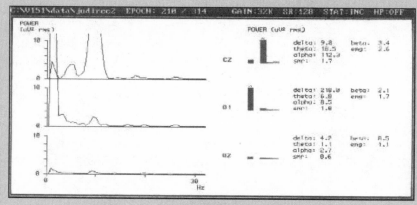

Post-Tachyon

The physical body is the last link in the energetic continuum of a human being. The body's metabolism is extremely complex and highly sensitive. Every disruption of metabolic processes can result in malfunctions, which can then manifest as dis-ease symptoms. Tachyonized materials, by creating order in the SOEFs, positively affect the metabolic process of the body. This phenomenon explains many questions that cannot be answered by a strictly biochemical examination of cellular metabolism. It serves to clarify, for example, how this incredibly complex mechanism can function with such precision.

The time has now come in which the practical use of Tachyonized materials for our spiritual development and perfect health in our entire body-mind complex is possible. Tachyonized materials enhance and accelerate our potential to become superconductors of the cosmic energy. The more powerfully cosmic energy moves through us, the more we are transformed into cosmic beings. The more we are unified on every level with the cosmic force, the more we are attuned to the divine in every moment. Tachyonized materials are not a replacement for a natural, spiritual lifestyle in harmony with all the natural laws of the planet. It is, however, the key to integrating and enhancing the balance and coherency needed on our path to perfect harmony with ourselves and all Creation. It is surely no coincidence that the utilization of Tachyonized materials is becoming possible at the end of the twentieth century.

CHAPTER 4

VERTICALITY–
THE RETURN HOME

A balanced development of consciousness on all levels of human life is less attainable with a horizontal, fragmented energy flow. Some strive to open the heart through dedication to God, others emphasize the opening of the third eye, while still others seek to experience God in the lower chakras. As spiritual awakening progresses, the seeker naturally becomes better able to reach a state of verticality during meditation. Most vertical states attained this way are normally only temporary, since the vertical system is not yet stabilized. Usually, within a few minutes to a few hours after meditation ends, the influence of other horizontal people or life situations overrides the verticality. The chakras once again adopt a horizontal position. Many spiritual aspirants, having some awareness of this issue, seek to limit their contact with worldly people as much as possible.

A stabilized vertical system in which we no longer are regularly pulled out of our connection with the divine by our horizontal world is the solution to this problem. Many paths, in one way or another, deal with an awakening where there is an energetic shift in consciousness. The most well-known form for this is known as the awakening of kundalini. In our framework this represents a major shift toward verticality.

The diagram on page 58 shows the typical horizontal energy system. With this system, a free flow of the life force through all chakras is limited or difficult. The life force, and therefore consciousness, can normally only be concentrated on

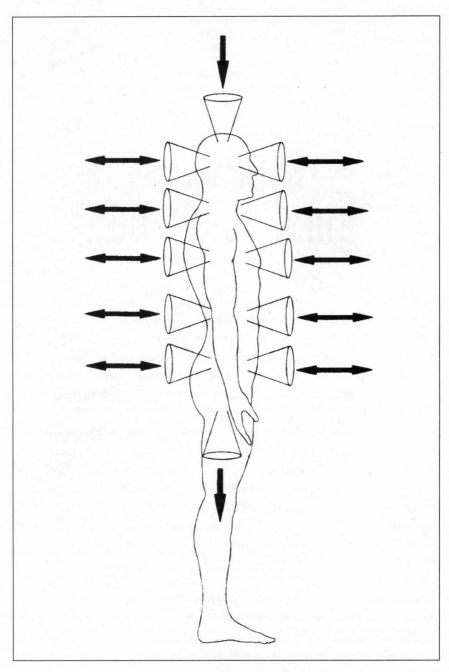

Diagram 1.
This diagram shows a horizontal system

one or at best two chakras. Because of this, the perception of ⸍
must inevitably be fragmented. He or she lives in the mind, in the ⸱
ven by his/her gut feelings. Life in all its fullness and diversity is thus
quently experienced.

KUNDALINI

There is an inborn evolutionary force that awakens as part of our spiritual evolution to bring us into verticality. In the yogic tradition this is called Kundalini. In
the Kabbalistic/Essene tradition it is called Ruach Hakodesh. In the Christian tradition it is referred to as the Holy Spirit. Since the term kundalini is almost uni-
versally used, we will use that terminology. Kundalini is the inherent inner force
that opens us to the ecstasy, love, and God awareness that is part of the transpersonal awakening, part of which we call verticalization. This is the most important
subtle energy system in terms of the spiritual evolution of the human species.
Carl Jung, in *Psychological Commentary on Kundalini*, said that "when you suc-
ceed in awakening the Kundalini, so that it starts to move out of its mere poten-
tiality, you necessarily start a world which is totally different from our world. It is
the world of eternity." Krishna, inspired by his own experience of kundalini
awakening, has written much to describe its meaning. He says of kundalini, "A
new center presently dormant in the average man and woman has to be activated
and a more powerful stream of psychic energy must rise into the head from the
base of the spine to enable human consciousness to transcend the normal limits.
This is the final phase of the present evolutionary impulse in man.... Here reason
yields to intuition and revelation appears to guide the steps of humankind.... This
mechanism, known as Kundalini, is the real cause of all genuine spiritual and
psychic phenomena, the biological basis of evolution and development of personality, the secret origin of all esoteric and occult doctrines, the master key to the
unsolved mystery of creation...."

Ramakrishna, considered by many to be one of the greatest Indian saints of
the last century, taught that an individual's spiritual consciousness is not awakened unless the kundalini is aroused. Swami Muktananda, a recent spiritual master in the yoga of kundalini who has awakened the kundalini energy in thousands
of spiritual hopefuls, said, "It is only when the Kundalini is awakened that we
become aware of our true nature, of our greatness." He points out that "as long as
the inner Kundalini is sleeping, it does not matter how many austerities we follow, how much yoga we practice . . . we will never realize our identity with our

ınner Self . . . The awakening of the inner Kundalini is the true beginning of the spiritual journey."

Although the various yoga traditions have been the main source of our detailed knowledge of kundalini in the West, a spiritualizing energy that seems to be the same as kundalini is acknowledged in many cultures. Katz, in the *Journal of Transpersonal Psychology,* describes how the Kung people of the Kalahari Desert in Northwest Botswana, Africa, danced for hours to awaken the *n/um* (kundalini) to attain the KIA state. He feels that the *n/um* is analogous to the kundalini and the KIA is a state of transcendence. He describes how about one half of the Kung people are able to heat up the *n/um*. In the Chinese Taoist tradition, Luk, in his book *Secret of Chinese Meditation,* describes an awakening process that is directly parallel to kundalini awakening. In the Christian tradition, Saint Terese of Lisieux, when she enrolled in a Carmelite convent at the age of ten, was reported to have had several months of spontaneous experiences with a "strange melange of hallucination, comas, and convulsions." Sometimes she had spontaneous movements such as springing from her knees and standing on her head without using her hands. Her history is compatible with descriptions of classical kundalini awakenings and also with those reported by Lee Sannella, M.D., in *Kundalini—Psychosis or Transcendence?* Kundalini and verticality are not, however, the same thing. When the kundalini is awakened, when a certain level of spiritual transformation has been achieved, verticality is one of the natural outcomes.

Becoming vertical in our energy flow is a way of accelerating our shift in consciousness. Through the use of a Tachyonized tool called the vortex pendant, there is a way to shift into a vertical state without necessarily having to awaken the kundalini. This allows many people to access the benefits of verticality without necessarily having spent much of one's life trying to awaken the kundalini. This is a boon to the spiritual seeker. When we're vertical we feel more "hooked in," more aligned with the cosmic process in our everyday lives. We have also found that the awakening of the kundalini is easier when people are vertical.

The point here is that through learning how to use Tachyonized materials, we can learn to restructure the system back to its natural verticality. This becomes one of the greatest gifts to us because usually the verticality experience in the spiritual path does not happen until a more advanced stage of the kundalini awakening. This gives the Tachyon practitioner a real opportunity to experience the wonderment of this higher-dimensional alignment in a way that acts as a divine feedback system so that he/she is encouraged to continue and evolve on the spiritual path. Verticality is a prerequisite for enlightenment. It is not enlightenment. At the end of the realization process and the full maturity of the kundalini, there is a permanent stabilization of the verticalization vortex. At the Quality of One workshop created by David Wagner, one learns to work with the vortex pendant and discovers techniques that help the verticalization process.

VERTICALITY—
BACK TO OUR NATURAL WAY OF BEING

All natural energy, such as trees, plants, animals, and most little children, possess a vertical energy system. The life force that forms consciousness flows vertically downward into the crown chakra, through all chakras, and returns upward via a three-dimensional loop located outside the body back into the crown chakra. The diagram on page 62 illustrates a tree's natural vertical energy flow.

Such a vertical system is completely balanced. The chakras have their flat sides facing upward and downward. All chakras are thus equally permeated by the life force; they are developed synchronously and are of equal size. As high as the life force reaches into the higher spheres is as deep as it is rooted in its vertical flow into the earth.

A baby normally comes into this world with its full connection to the divine. One manifestation of this vertical chakra system is the continual vertical energy flow, where the energy of the divine moves fully and continuously through the baby. When the baby's spirit first enters the womb, its vertical state is so strong that it actually helps attune the mother, and oftentimes the father, to a vertical system. So there is a sense of well-being and joy and a glow that we often see in both women and couples that are pregnant. When the baby is born, the temporary verticalization of the parents shifts back to the horizontal pattern. At some point of the maturation process, in the process of acclimating to this world and being in the family, the baby loses this overwhelming connection with the divine and consequently shifts from the vertical to a horizontal chakra system. This represents in essence a partial disconnection from the awareness of the divine presence. Practically speaking, in terms of the chakra systems, all the chakras except the root and crown turn horizontal.

The evolutionary challenge we are addressing with Tachyonized materials is how to shift the horizontal system back to its natural vertical pattern and thus enhance our communion with the divine being in the world. This would create a new possibility. If the parents were stable vertical beings prior to conception, the

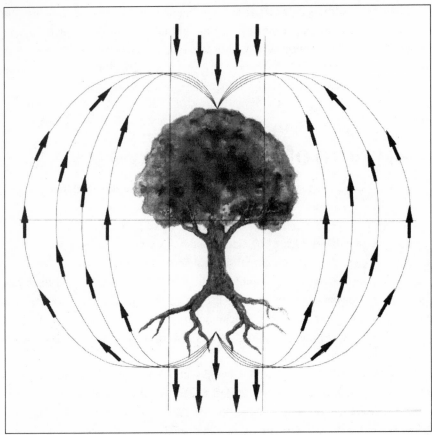

Diagram 2.
This diagram shows the natural vertical energy as it flows through the tree.

communion of the whole family with the divine would be enhanced by their baby's birth, and the baby would most likely not switch to a horizontal system. Vertical families attuned to All That Is could possibly shift the very consciousness of the planet.

A friend of mine who teaches yoga likes to tell the following story at her seminars. A friend of hers already had a four-year-old son when she gave birth to her second child. The four-year-old always wanted to be close to his young brother. The mother, puzzled by his behavior, finally asked him why he was so fond of his tiny brother. The child replied, "I ask him what it is like to live with God, because I am about to forget." This incident gives an indication of the loss involved in spontaneously shifting from vertical to horizontal.

In verticality, with all the chakras being open to the natural vertical flow of the divine, all the chakras become integrated. (See Diagram 3 on page 64.) This, in turn, helps us become integrated at every level of our being. So we are open not only to the divine as it flows through, but also all those different aspects of consciousness that are stored in each chakra. For example, higher love in the heart chakra, sexuality and creativity in the second chakra. In the horizontal system, the chakras and all their different aspects of consciousness are not integrated. The result is we have physical, emotional, and mental fragmentation. And although we may awaken a particular chakra, or activate it at a certain point, there isn't the integration that you have in the vertical flow system, so you do not have that continual integration of the personality and of the physical, mental, emotional and spiritual aspects. In verticality, the energy flows down through the entire body, through each chakra, and extends down deep into the earth, connecting you with the very soil and blood of the earth; then it loops around to the heavens. This movement creates a communion with your entire environment, which in turn opens you up to communion with the divine. What has happened in our society is that we've become so horizontal that we have broken our connections with the heavens and the earth and have begun to act in a disconnected way. Being disconnected not only creates poor health and disharmony but directly contributes to a consciousness that allows the continual destruction of the Earth and all her life.

Part of healing the planet is the reconnection to the vertical flow. Once you know and feel communion with these things, you begin treating the planet, animals, and plants in a way that reflects that communion. If everyone were vertical, we would not have wars, nor could we continue to destroy our planet. Therefore, the implications of verticality on the planet are very significant. In essence, verticality tunes us into what we call the lover's lifestyle, where you're feeling love for yourself and all of creation on a regular unbroken basis. In that love relationship we do everything we can to enhance and enliven the plants, animals, the planet, and all relationships with all human beings.

Verticalization has been described in many systems. In the Kabbalah it is known as the *shekhina* energy, or the feminine face of God. *Shekhina* refers to life-force energy and spirit within all of creation that flows down into us. It refers to all energies, and all frequencies that exist—all of life. The feminine face of God is considered the presence of the divine in all of creation. The masculine, which is known as the *EinSof* in the Kabbalah or *Shiva* in the yogic system, is a state where there is no form and there is no flowing energy, there is only existence. The resurrection of the *shekhina* energy, or the *Shakti* energy, is needed in our awareness for the healing of the planet and ourselves. When it is awake in us, we see and feel the life force within ourselves and then evolve to see and feel it in all people, animals, plants, and the living planet itself. As we honor this energy and elevate it, it reconnects and brings us into balance with all that is.

Verticalization is the awakening and reconnecting process that aligns us with the cosmic feminine within us, whether we are male or female. *Shiva* and *Shakti* are two sides of one coin. Tachyon energy is the middle of the coin connecting the two. Because it is without frequency, it represents the masculine, and because it has form and is measurable, it also represents the feminine. It is the integration point between the two. All energy on this planet (all of creation) is considered feminine in relationship to the formless masculine energy of the *EinSof*, *Shiva*, or zero-point. Ultimately there is no masculine or feminine, but we use these metaphorical terms to help describe the play of the universe.

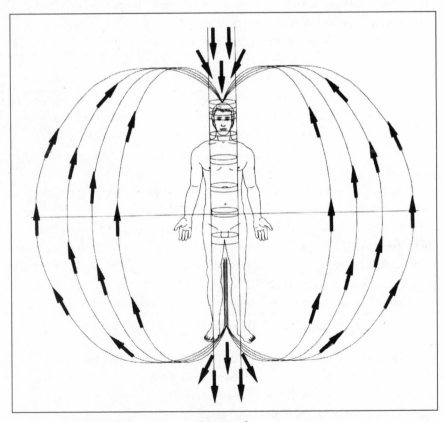

Diagram 3.
This diagram shows an integrated vertical system.

KUNDALINI VORTEX

The terms verticalization and verticalizing the chakras were coined by David Wagner, the inventor of the Tachyonization process, which will be described later. Verticalization in yogic terms is described by Gabriel Cousens, M.D. in his book *Spiritual Nutrition and the Rainbow Diet,* as part of the evolution of the Kundalini process and of awakening.

In this kundalini process, the SOEFs become more and more organized as the energy is drawn up. Our body tends to become more etheric. The increasingly energized kundalini vortex transmutes more matter and more energy from the more dense subtle energy systems until the subtle energy of the whole organism is drawn into one energy vortex. As the energy naturally begins to flow downward we literally become one and experience ourselves as whole and complete. An experiential reminder of this is the almost continual awareness of oneself as a single vertical transcendent energy field resonating with and being drawn back into the cosmic energy vibration. This vertical resonating and merging experience, particularly during periods of silent meditation, seems to penetrate to the very atomic level of one's being.

At the time of the kundalini awakening, the chakras and the subtle bodies become absorbed into the more purified powerful energy of the kundalini vortex. Enough of the chakra energy is left to maintain us on the physical plane, but the chakras lose their predominant role and significance. What is left is the continual experience of the pulsation of the pure prana flowing down through the kundalini vortex. This becomes the central energy source of the physical system. The crown chakra changes at kundalini, awakening from a minor portal of energy entry to that of the most important source of energy in the system. The whole system thus reaches a higher level of SOEF organization and provides a model that explains the process of resurrection. It may also explain the passage in John 20:17, in which Jesus says to Mary Magdalene, "Stop clinging to me. For I have not yet ascended to the father." In John 20:19 and John 20:26, Jesus passes through the locked doors of his disciples' dwellings to bless them with peace. What may be happening is that Jesus' SOEF was so highly organized and his physical structure so nearly transmuted into the etheric level that he was able to go the next step and make his body totally etheric by the use of his mind. This would allow him to pass through locked doors. By projecting his mind down into the vortex, he could draw up the materials needed into the SOEF to repattern and recreate his own body as needed to serve the will of God. This is a theoretical extension of our total vortex and SOEF aspects of our new holistic paradigm.

The shift from horizontal to vertical existence can be described in terms of minimizing the horizontal chakra system and maximizing the shift to vertical kundalini. Here is a quotation from a liberated spiritual teacher who describes his verticalization process in yogic terms in *Spiritual Nutrition and the Rainbow Diet:*

Ever since the forty-day fast, I feel as if I am wearing a pulsating skullcap all the time and the top of my crown chakra has been cut off like the bottom of the skullcap, and the divine energy is intensely pouring in through it. Muktananda, I believe, would refer to this continual pranic crown chakra pulsation when he occasionally mentioned in public lectures that he breathed through the sushumna. Da Love Ananda (Da Free John), I believe, refers to his transcendent shift to a central vortex energy predominance and the absorption of the basic chakra energy into this central vortex, when he describes his experience. He felt that the topmost part of his crown chakra was severed and the life current, another name for kundalini, was no longer bound to the chakras as a necessary structure. This experience of crown chakra severing and subtle cosmic pranic pulsation is a direct inner and outer total transcendent harmonic connection with the pure cosmic vibration. It is but another reminder of our true formless reality. It is the ultimate food for transcendence. It is the delicacy of spiritual nutrition. It is food from God and the energy of God as God. The unitary kundalini vortex is so energized by the cosmic prana that we are transformed into shining vortexual bodies of light. It is a basis for understanding the subtle meaning of Exodus 34:28 and 29, "So he was there with the Lord 40 days and 40 nights; he neither ate bread, nor drank water. ... Now it was so, when Moses came down from Mount Sinai (and the two tablets of the Testimony were in Moses' hand when he came down from the mountain), that Moses did not know that the skin of his face shown while he talked with Him."

Transcendence is the evolutionary process by which the vortexual energy of the Kundalini progressively transmutes us from the gross matter of our bodies to a more refined and highly organized and energized SOEF. It is the physical parallel to the transmutation of our consciousness to the Love of unity awareness. Eventually it takes us into complete absorption of our form into the formless energies of God. From the time the kundalini is awakened, we gradually become more etheric, but even after the total merging of the kundalini energies, enough of our physical body and chakra system is left so we can function in the world. My lack of direct experience beyond this point does not allow me to go much further in our discussion. It is the process of transcendence, which explains the physical transcendence of Tukaram, Elijah, Enoch, and Jesus. Our spiritual potentials are awesome. This physical transcendence is not necessarily the goal of spiritual life as much as it represents a total freedom to follow God's will. In any case, whatever happens, it is enough just to ... be."

Creating the Vortex Pendant

Short of the intense commitment required for the enlightenment process, which few people are able to make, David Wagner postulated that there must be a way to help people move back into their natural vertical state. In this state they may begin to experience the joy and peace of divine communion.

Since he was a youth, David had observed the fragmented way that humans operate on an energetic level. With his ability to see energy move, it was blatantly obvious that, for the most part, humans experience life energetically disconnected from the source. Compounding this limitation is the fact that the human fragmented system is capable of only moving energy into one chakra and out of another. A simple example is the experience of love. Most people are experts at giving or sending love to their world. Unfortunately it is extremely difficult for a horizontal system to both receive and send love simultaneously. For this reason most people find an imbalance in their capacity to receive love, when compared to their proficiency in giving love. Only giving from one center leads to an experience of imbalance and a sense of disconnectedness. What if the source of love vanishes? We are once again left hollow or empty. Unable to replenish ourselves with divine love, we begin to search out another source of love, once again, looking outside of ourselves. This is the root of a global human experience, the sense of separation from God. If the human energy system were restored to its original vertical flow, then the human experience would change back into one of integration and unification with All That Is, creating peace on Earth.

Early in David's life he began establishing and testing methods that could harmonize and verticalize the human energy system. Finally in 1986, David began to teach his method for verticalizing and restoring harmony. The results were mixed. The students experienced verticality, but their "real" world always proved to be too much and the system re-horizontalized, usually within days. The missing element was the ability to maintain a vertical energy system, particularly when exposed to the unconscious energy piracy of horizontal people and other weakening influences of our human environment.

Most people in this world have experienced the constant energy depletion of our environment, of our social interaction with people, pollution, stress, and electromagnetic fields. Even the very foods we eat can have a depleting effect on us rather than an energy-increasing effect. The end result of this is that it's very hard to get out of the horizontally based world and into a vertically aligned system with the ability to experience the infinite energy flow of the divine. Of course you could retreat to a cave or a special place removed from society—a favorite practice of many traditions. Most people, however, do not have or cannot afford the many years needed to devote to such practices, or they realize that at this time in history our work is to elevate and heal the planet rather than to escape from it. The path of verticality is bringing spirit back into the world. Verticality helps us spiritualize our own consciousness and all those around us. The more people who become vertical, the more effect we have in transforming and healing the world. Verticality is not the same as enlightenment; it is, however, a prerequisite for enlightenment.

David, realizing that verticality is a precondition of enlightenment, found himself continually searching for a global answer that would assist or create a vertical energy flow free of frequency influences. And then it happened! Three years after he invented the Tachyonization machines, David had a clear and perfect revelation that began a revolution in verticality. The beauty is that helping people become vertical supports the shift of consciousness toward enlightenment.

This breakthrough included the invention of a new tool called a Tachyonized vortex pendant. The vortex pendant actually stabilizes and maintains verticality. It is the only tool of its kind. No frequency tool or frequency method of verticalizing the system could possibly do the work of a Tachyonized vortex pendant. The vortexual energy created through verticality is a continual balance of cosmic energy that maintains and evolves the entire body-mind emotional and spiritual complex. This is something no frequency can do. Remember that a frequency will push the body into balance and then out. Frequencies have no intelligence. Because of the profound effects this tool has, it is not made available to the general public. But since 1993, clinical studies and the monitoring of thousands of people using this tool have proven that the process works!

The Quality of One seminars provide individuals with all the necessary background information and techniques to benefit from the Tachyonized vortex pendant. These tools make it possible to make a safe transition from a horizontal-based system of losing and usurping energy into a vertical energy system that is completely self-contained and connected to All That Is. By having the necessary tools to help with the clearing of the emotional, mental, and physical blocks, students found the transition to be a fairly smooth one. The outcome is the realization that verticality is absolutely natural. Verticality opens the doorway to help us adopt a lifestyle that adheres to the cosmic order and the natural laws of life.

RELATIONSHIPS AND SEXUALITY

Being vertical opens one up to new dynamics in relationships. Verticality allows for a deep, intimate connection because it enhances the experience of all levels of another person in all the energy centers of the vertical person. As a vertical energy system entrains or interacts with any energy system, whether it be an animal or a tree, the entire available energy can be experienced vertically in every chakra center. In a personal relationship, the depth and quality of understanding among friends enhances the relationship. Between lovers, verticality allows for the fullest level of contact, integration and the experience of oneness. Because verticality increases the direct experience of divine love and communion, it minimizes codependency patterns. It strengthens the depth of the bonding and will deepen and strengthen joy in life. As the shift happens, the newly verticalized person still has buttons that can be pushed. Being vertical doesn't mean there will be no problems in shedding dysfunctional behavioral patterns. In the Quality of One workshop, tools have been developed specifically to enhance the dissolving of unconscious and conscious behavior patterns. The peace and completeness from a vertical state helps us lose our fear of intimacy, which is one of the main reasons people have problems in relationships. Sharing our inner joy with other people becomes a life-enriching process. Verticality gives us the opportunity of attaining total inner peace and freedom. Whether we choose to use it is up to us. Verticality is accessible for every person, regardless of his or her religious or spiritual background. In all religious prophecies a quantum leap in the spiritual growth of humanity is predicted. As long as we live with a horizontal system, such a quantum leap is an arduous and time-consuming proposition. Verticality presents every spiritual aspirant with the opportunity to return to unity with God and Creation in this lifetime, and thus play a part in the fulfillment of the old prophecies.

All religious teachings emphasize that spiritual growth enables a person to see God in all living beings, and to live in this connectedness. As long as there is no consciousness of connectedness, people will even manipulate the most perfect outer system. If, however, we awaken into the unity behind diversity in Creation, we will realize that all people and all beings are a part of our own true Self. Verticality significantly enhances this awareness.

Living in connectedness also means becoming aware of the consequences of our lifestyle. For many people, one of the most significant consequences of such awareness is the transition to a vegetarian lifestyle. Vegetarianism is an important contribution to the harmony of the world, a world in which we as human beings respect our brothers and sisters of the nonhuman kingdom as fellow beings of equal value. We thus no longer view them as resources that may be sacrificed in great numbers for a superficial consumption that not only harms our health but also creates a hoarding and misuse of resources, which harms the planet.

Verticality is of great benefit in experiencing a profound connectedness with all life. With a vertically aligned energy system we become more receptive to the inner being of other people, as well as to the pulsating life energy of nature. We reach a state of inner completeness, which replaces the need for outer struggles and the longing for superficial prestige. Verticality helps us become pure instruments for true love.

Verticality diminishes our susceptibility to, and thus our fear of negative influences. This naturally leads to a greater freedom in life. When the chakra energy system shifts to vertical, all our energy centers can be continuously fed by our vertical connection with the planet, nature, and our energetic continuum. Since we experience everything on all levels, and as connectedness and unity strengthen us, we begin to lose our fear. This is a relatively quick process with the use of certain techniques in conjunction with the vortex pendant.

In the world as most of us know it, humans often rely on the energy of other humans. In the vertical world you have no need for the energy of others. In fact, there is so much energy flowing through a vertical system that you begin to heal and nurture the planet just by your very being. As we develop an integrated vertical system we enhance our access to all of nature and the cosmic energies that flow through everything. We begin to radiate this love and peace, and all those who would usurp energy from us are now fed the inexhaustible energy of love and peace flowing through us. This, for many, is healing and balancing in itself. From the vertical experience there is never a depletion of energy, since it is the only system that is completely self-sufficient and that fills us with the energy of love and peace.

CHAPTER 5

HEALING WITH TACHYON

In order to appreciate and truly understand the principles of healing with tachyon, it is helpful to review briefly the vibrational healing theories of holistic medicine. The vibrational approach includes such therapies as: orgone therapy, magnetic field therapy, radionics, bioresonance therapy, photon energy, homeopathy, healing work with crystals, color therapy, flower and gem elixirs, sound therapy, and much more. Frequencies are further complicated by individualized oscillations and right or left spins. All these methods are based on one common principle: within our energetic continuum of subtle bodies, obstructions can manifest on any frequency level, and these obstructions then cause health problems. If one supplies the affected subtle frequency level with strengthening and harmonizing energy of its own frequency, these impediments can be dissolved and the state of health improved.

Properly applied, the use of energies with specific frequencies can lead to excellent results if in fact people know what frequency they are dealing with. Yet all such methods have two significant drawbacks that are unavoidable.

The first drawback is the effects of energy with a specific frequency, as used in vibrational medicine, are mostly limited to the range of that frequency. Photon energy, for example, is described as packets of light energy. Scientists use this concept to refer to the particle-like aspects of light. Photons are always associated with an electromagnetic wave of a definite frequency. There currently are frequency energy tools that emit photon energy from the far-infrared spectrum between 4 and 16 (micrometers) wavelength, which is a small electromagnetic wave of the total frequency possibility of photon energy. This narrow frequency does correspond to a frequency in the auric body. If there were a blockage in this narrow frequency range there would be a deficiency of energy between the blocked level and the physical body. But what if the blockage lies between 18 and 35 micrometers? Applying this photon energy frequency might have some indirect influence, but it surely would not clear the blockage from, nor could it reconnect the system to, the energetic continuum. So, one of the significant drawbacks to energetic medicine is that you need to know exactly at what frequency the blockage is in order to apply the right frequency.

All subtle therapeutic methods other than tachyon do not enhance our attunement with zero-point energy, but only with isolated frequencies of the whole. Accessing the complete spectrum of frequency and information to clear the entire system and restore total functionality of our energetic continuum is very rare and difficult using a single-frequency approach because people may have multiple blocks at different frequencies.

The second drawback is that energies of a specific frequency can also have harmful effects. There are two basic reasons for this: an excess of any frequency can potentially be just as harmful as an energy deficiency; and because a frequency has no intelligence, the user needs wisdom, insight, and training to determine the actual exposure time and specific frequency that is needed. A simple example may help illuminate the point. The sun is a magnificent source of photon energy. Approximately twenty to thirty exposure minutes per day are necessary for optimum health. Yet this same ball of photon energy will burn you to a crisp if you spend three or four hours in a hot tropical sun. Photon energy, like all frequencies, has no intelligence and doesn't know when to start or stop! So it is up to the user to decide when to stop the exposure. Another example is excess exposure to orgone energy. We know that orgone energy can be used as a positive energy. But orgone energy, just like all slower-than-light energies, is a frequency. And as a frequency, orgone energy has also been shown to be able to push the body out of balance, making it very sick. It is a common fact that orgone energy can be transformed into a negative force field that can have disastrous effects on the body. But this is simply the nature of frequencies. These simple examples are meant to give you an insight into the difficulties inherent in and the mixed results that are often obtained from frequency-oriented medicine.

This explains why a magnet only works on certain things and why its misuse is cause for alarm. In fact, one common question is, what is the difference between Tachyonized materials and magnetic energy? Magnets work on a specific frequency, with the North and South Poles having opposite effects. The South Pole is activating. If it is used for too long, it can create a hyperactivity in the system and cause harm. For example, some people using magnetic mattresses developed high blood pressure, which fortunately went away when they were told to stop using the magnetic mattress. This can happen because magnets operate on a frequency and have intensity, but do not have built-in intelligence to know when to stop broadcasting.

Tachyon is not a frequency, nor is it a frequency approach. Frequency, oscillation, or spin do not exist at the level at which Tachyon operates. Its effects are regulated by the internal wisdom of the SOEFs. When Tachyonized materials are applied to an area, the SOEFs convert exactly what they need to restore themselves to perfect balance and order.

The following research demonstrates the balancing and potential healing effects of Tachyon as measured in both Europe and the United States.

ELECTRO-DIAGNOSTIC RESEARCH ON MERIDIAN RESPONSE TO TACHYONIZED WATER IN HUMANS

The number "50" represents ideal organ or system function in this electro-diagnostic system. A reading above 65 indicates that the organ or system, as measured through its corresponding meridian point, is in a state of energetic imbalance. The

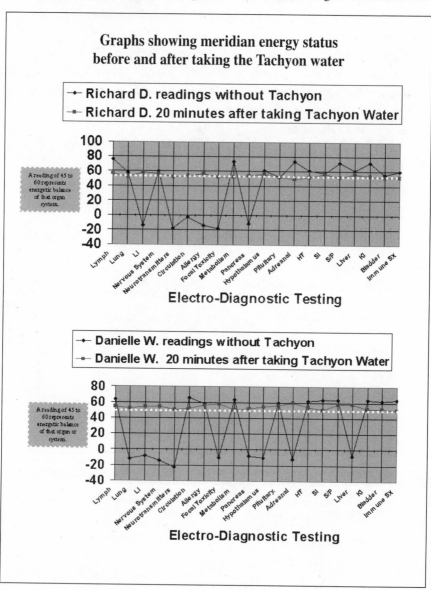

further the reading is from 50, the greater the imbalance. Drops in the amplitude or scores of 10 points less than 50 meridian points show where there is a significant energy drain or leak. In these instances, the body is losing life-force energy on an electromagnetic level, potentially creating a serious problem.

These graphs show different clients before and after meridian readings.

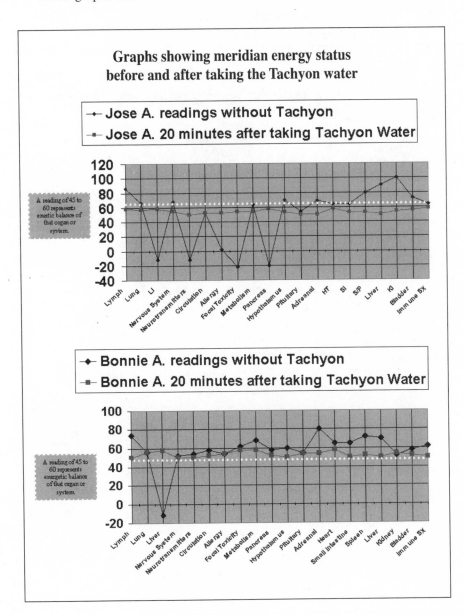

The diamond studded lines are the control readings. The square studded line shows the readings 20 minutes after 20 drops of Tachyonized water was taken sublingually

This reaserch indicates the Tachyonized materials effected all imbalanced

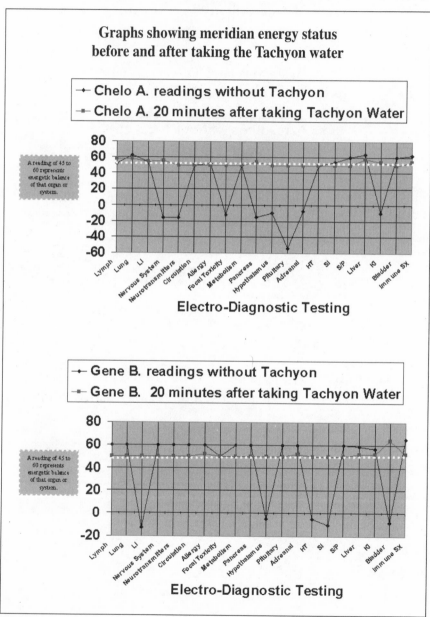

meridians, creating an energetic balance no one frequency could accomplish. It is vital for the organs and glands to be energetically balanced in order to create physical balance. We clearly see the youthing or neg-entropic effects Tachyonized water has on the energetic system.

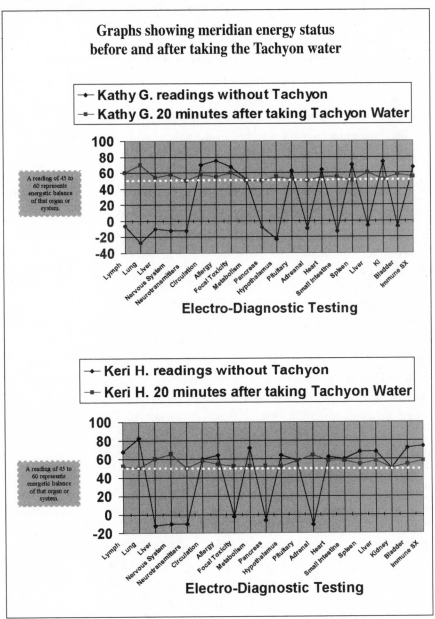

PROGNOS

Prognos was developed in connection with Russian projects researching the effects of long-term space travel on humans. The results of sixteen years of scientific research and development were used in identifying Tachyonized materials effects.

During the Prognos diagnosis, the skin resistance is measured at the initial and final points of the meridians on the hands and feet.

The relevant data is automatically transferred to the computer system, where it is processed by a sophisticated program. The assessment performed by the program is based on millions of reference measurements. The final readout is a graphic representation of the meridian's state of balance.

The graphs chart:
- the total energy of the test person,
- the balance of yin/yang as well as the upper/lower part and the left/right side of the body, and
- the interrelationship of the client's organ-meridians system.

The graphs give a holistic survey of the energy resources of the test person and thus provide valuable diagnostic information.
- Alterations in the condition of an organ-meridian system are displayed (possibly) before symptoms appear so that therapeutic intervention can prevent serious consequences.
- Although this diagnostic system was originally designed to be used with traditional acupuncture, Tachyonized materials proved to quickly affect both the left and right side of the body, rebalancing the meridians-organs energetically.

Prognos is very accurate. The measurement data is reproducible with low variations. Several measurements can be performed in one day or over a period of time.

The graph on page 79 is one of many provided by Dr. Simble. The purpose of the study was to identify how Tachyonized materials affected the meridian system. Several important insights can be derived from the data presented: Tachyonized materials brought all twenty-four points back into a complete state of balance. This infers that Tachyon is either an extremely large frequency bandwidth or is actually not a frequency. To identify which of these two were true, cells were taped on for extended periods of time. If Tachyon were in fact a frequency, the meridians would be forced out of balance within a few hours or days.

The cells were left on for thirteen days! The graph below shows the results. All twenty-four meridians achieved energetic balance and stayed there. The conclusion was that Tachyonized materials from Advanced Tachyon Technologies provide the energetic body with the right energy to move back into balance and stay there—something no frequency can do.

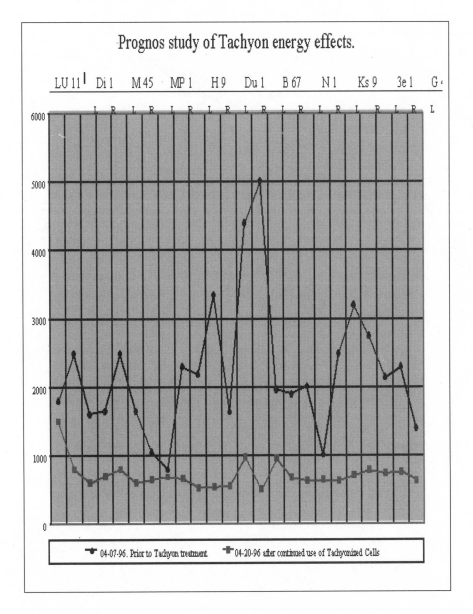

When SOEFs are brought into balance, they automatically begin to function normally as they stop converting tachyon into SOEF organization. The key is that the tachyon energy works at the SOEF level where this body-wisdom feedback loop exists. *Vibrational medicine does not work at the SOEF level and doesn't have the benefit and safety of the SOEF feedback loop in the healing process.*

DARK-FIELD STUDY OF LIVE BLOOD
By Gabriel Cousens, M.D.

Live-blood research conducted in Germany by researchers Joerg Rinne, HP and Peter Thomas found several significant results in this preliminary study. We would like to share two of these findings here. Using a dark-field microscope, they documented the effects Tachyonized water has on live blood. One observation was that red blood cell clumping was reversed within forty-five minutes. This confirmed Dr. Cousens' earlier dark-field study showing the same results in ten out of ten people. The second finding was that Tachyonized water maintained the life force of the blood for at least eight hours in the same blood that had previously degenerated and decayed, losing its life force before the eight hours.

They were quite satisfied that this preliminary research demonstrated Tachyonized water's substantial life-enhancing effects. These photos document some of their findings and are excerpts from their original research project.

In this study human blood life-force serves as an intrinsic indicator for the qualitative changes induced by Tachyon Energy. The implications once again support our theories that Tachyon energy unequivocally effects the SOEFs, thereby increasing their energy and ability to maintain neg-entropy and hence retain life-force and form observed as cellular integrity.

Though frequency-oriented treatments have become common today, many users are not made aware of the potential drawbacks. Yet even with these limitations, frequency-oriented medicine has proven to be one of our best tools for creating balance without drugs until now! Tachyon energy is free of these problems and offers an even safer approach.

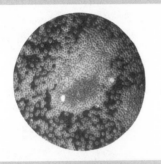

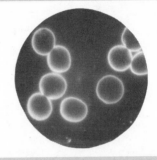

In Photo One the client's blood is taken prior to any exposure to Tachyonized materials. Clumping of the erythrocytes can be seen.

Photo Two is of the same person's blood, taken 45 minutes after the sublingual absorption of 15 drops of Tachyonized water. Already improved, the erythrocytes are singular and free in the plasma.

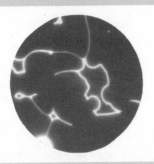

Photo Three is the same blood as Photo One. The difference here is that eight hours have elapsed and the blood is dead! Only cell fragments are r ecognizable.

Photo Four is the same blood as in Photo Two. After eight hours you can see the blood is still alive and the cells still have their cellular integrity.

TACHYON HEALING

There are several keys to tachyon healing: tachyon energy is the source of all frequencies; tachyon energy is not a frequency; tachyon energy directly energizes the SOEF, whereas frequencies do not; and tachyon contains all the potential of our entire energetic continuum. These are the four basic principles of tachyon healing. This wholeness makes the effects of tachyon energy healing treatment universal and without side effects. You do not need to know what frequency is needed since all frequencies are potentials inside tachyon. Tachyon energy is negentropic, which means it reverses entropic degeneration and can only create order in the system. When tachyon energy is applied, you do not need to know when to stop its application, because it reorganizes and restructures the SOEFs. When the SOEFs reach their maximum structure, they can't go any further and so the healing effect of the tachyon energy ends. A side benefit of using Tachyonized materials over energetic medicine is that when practitioners maintain a constant flow of tachyon energy through their own systems, it is extremely unusual to take on the clients' energies.

Since tachyons do not have a specific frequency, they are not affected by gravity. Since they are not affected by gravity, they do not have a gravitational pull. No frequency matrix can hold or transfer tachyon energy. It cannot be broadcast with radionics devices because radionics devices only transmit frequency matrices, and, again, tachyon is not a frequency and cannot be stored or transmitted through a frequency matrix. The fact is, *nothing can transmit tachyon energy.*

Tachyonized materials are *antennas* that are able to draw and concentrate the tachyon energy out of the omnipresent, infinite, zero-point energy. It is a totally different energetic potential principle. Tachyon energy can be used to directly charge the SOEFs of any living system or material, but *"charging" is not the same as the Tachyonization process.* For example, water can be charged by placing Tachyonized material in the water or on the container. Doing this will raise the bioenergetic potential of the water, increasing and balancing the SOEFs to their highest level, but it does not change the water at the submolecular level, and therefore does not change it into a tachyon antenna: Tachyonized water is extremely different from charged water because it has been restructured at the submolecular level through the fourteen-day Tachyonization process. This converts the water molecules into permanent antennas for tachyon energy. When they are consumed, they disburse as tachyon antennas in the form of water molecules throughout the body. This has a very beneficial effect, as we have demonstrated.

We highly recommend charging water with Tachyonized material so that the water you are consuming is at its highest water vibration potential.

With tachyon energy, the entire complex of subtle and physical levels of the energetic continuum receives access to all potential that is needed for self-healing. For every energy obstruction, disharmony, energy deficiency, or lack of order in our body-mind complex, we can find the suitable solution through Tachyonized materials. The point is that the tachyon energy through the energetic continuum re-organizes, re-structures and energizes all levels of the subtle organized energy fields from the subtle body levels, to the cellular level, to the organ and tissue level and ultimately, to the cellular organizing field for the total organism. In this way, it creates a multi-dimensional healing impact and anti-aging treatment. As these fields become structured, the body goes into unity, harmony and health. That is how the tachyon energy works. Because it is self-regulating, tachyon healing is easier to learn than many other techniques, yet is still incredibly effective. In fact, the Tachyon Practitioner Course takes only a few days to complete.

Since our body-mind complex decides itself which effects it permits, the results of applying tachyon energy are always positive. It is possible, however, to apply so much tachyon to an energetic system that it begins to work very well and thus begins to detoxify. When this happens you may feel physical and sometimes emotional detoxification, which is a natural part of the healing process and therefore very positive. For the unprepared, however, this could be perceived as negative. Nonetheless, tachyon energy creates order out of disorder and harmful effects are not possible. Research from around the world has provided clinical results showing that tachyon energy is 75 to 90 percent effective in the reduction or relief of all types of physical pain. These results are even more encouraging when one takes into account that most clients have tried numerous other modalities prior to discovering tachyon energy.

ELECTRONIC MUSCLE TESTER AND TACHYON

The objective of the next study was to determine if Tachyonized materials, when applied to specific organs or glands that were underactive or overactive, could be tested using an electronic muscle tester (EMT). The EMT is a development in technology that brings the useful technique of muscle testing into the area of scientific measurement. This might provide insight into whether Tachyonized materials would strengthen or weaken the body complex.

The technique of testing the strength or weakness of a muscle has been taught to chiropractors for many years. George Goodhart, D.C., has been one of the chief proponents. When the client puts a finger on a particular gland or organ and the muscle nearest it is tested, that muscle will normally test weaker in strength when the gland or organ is malfunctioning.

For example, if a person is fighting an infection, the thymus gland (just under the throat) may be underactive. If a Tachyonized cell is applied to the thymus gland, any muscle will show an increase in strength. In other words, the Tachyonized cell quickly affects the body. If the same test is done without the Tachyonized cell on the thymus, the muscles would probably test significantly weaker.

Practically any organ or gland or muscle group can be tested. The test depends on measurement of the muscle strength, or of some muscle group strength. Often one of the muscles in the arm is used, but the finger muscles are sometimes quicker and simpler to use. This testing usually requires a second person to push or pull on the muscle. The person's judgment of muscle strength may be a necessary part of the procedure, which is a disadvantage because it brings a subjective component to the procedure that sometimes makes accuracy difficult.

Although there are ways to self-test, it is not easy nor is it a sure way to attain accurate results, because again the individual may be biased in one direction or the other.

EMT eliminates the need for another person to do the test. It is more objective and simpler to use. Of course, it is still not 100 percent objective, because motivation, intention, determination, and bias may influence the results. However, it is a significant advancement in muscle-testing procedures because it can be used by anyone anywhere.

In order to select test subjects that had no previous affinity for Tachyonized materials, we set up our research station at the Whole Life Exposition in New York and tested over 200 subjects. Using a blind method of testing, we eliminated most subjectivity. The participants were shown how the EMT worked, and once they were ready, the meter was shielded from their view. This eliminated their contribution to the results they thought they wanted. After developing a baseline the participant would hold, wear, or cover their troubled area with Tachyonized materials.

Results were always consistent. In all but a few cases we found that applying Tachyonized materials to a specific organ, gland, or muscle group caused an increase in physical strength measured by the EMT. It is important to note that

5/200 people we tested had no marked increase in strength. There were also 3/200 people who were initially weaker when we applied Tachyonized materials. In all three cases we found that using a smaller cell always resulted in an increase in energy strength. We believe that this was the result of the body's absorption and utilization of the energy, which in all three cases if provided in large quantities would have caused a large physical detoxification, in our opinion. In many cases we had to switch to a higher scale in order to accurately record the new readings. Approximately fifteen individuals reacted so strongly to the Tachyonized materials that the EMT was not able to give us a top reading. Quite amazing was the fact that the EMT was able to accurately identify the body's desire (whether mental, emotional, or physical) to heal or detoxify.

We found size to be of importance. It seemed that the whole area needed to be covered with Tachyonized materials to achieve the maximum EMT reading. Below is a small sampling of the data accumulated.

To achieve accurate readings, the baseline is always adjusted as close to zero as possible. For this reason all graphed readings referenced start at zero.

Of the 200 people tested to see the effect of Tachyonized cells on body strength, 97.5 percent tested stronger and 2.5 percent showed no increase in strength.

This study demonstrates the body's quick response to the balancing effects of Tachyonized materials. The EMT measured the SOEF's conversion of tachyon into usable biological energy. This biological energy, when not being used for strength, would naturally be used by the body to heal and rejuvenate the areas covered with the tachyon antenna.

A few people have reported that they have an initial sense of being overenergized by the Tachyonized materials. These people are not used to operating at a higher integrated energetic potential, which is exactly what happens with the use of Tachyonized tools. After a short period of time, everyone readjusts and becomes comfortable operating at a higher level of integration. This is a very positive effect. For many healings there are physical changes that can be felt.

Tachyon energy is holistic in that it enhances a person's potential to heal on any level of the energetic continuum. It does this by the direct reorganizing of the SOEFs, which helps clear the blocks in the energy continuum responsible for the energy deficiency of the underlying systems. Blocks can happen in any of the mental, emotional, physical, or spiritual bodies, and clearing a blockage in one body will reorganize that level and normally result in the completion of the healing process.

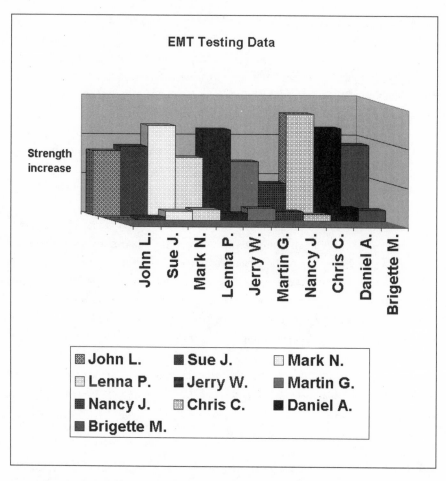

Another insight into the tachyon dynamics of healing is seen through the example of what happens to people when they fast: their psycho-physiological defenses begin to melt away, their ability to access imbalances and blockages improves, and psycho-physiological healing is accelerated. Tachyon energy, by helping you become more attuned to the higher levels of who you are, makes it easier to clear and let go of mental, emotional, physical, and spiritual blocks. If Tachyonized materials are used as part of your verticalization attunement, your vibration rate could rise to the point where many lower-vibrational blocks cannot stay in your system due to your higher vibration.

Through tachyon, the entire complex of subtle and physical levels of the energetic continuum receives access to all information that is needed for self-healing. For every energy obstruction, disharmony, energy deficiency, or lack of order in our body-mind complex, the suitable solution can be found through tachyon energy.

Tachyon energy enables attunement with cosmic zero-point energy. It is therefore much easier upon reaching a bifurcation point to move through the bifurcation point into a new octave of health, harmony, and spiritual awakening. Entropy, decreased order, and aging are transformed into neg-entropy, increased order, and reversal of aging, allowing the entire system to move in a positive direction.

Tachyon energy creates unified energy fields. This leads to one of the many exciting applications for tachyon: electromagnetic fields (EMFs) created by alternating current are very common today in our world of technological overkill and may have harmful effects upon our health. But such electromagnetic fields lose their negative effects when they become coherent through the unified field of tachyon. Electrosmog emitted from electrical devices in the household, screen radiation of computers, and geopathic stress factors can be neutralized to a large degree through tachyon.

CHAPTER 6

EXPERIMENTS WITH LIVE ORGANISMS

FRUIT FLIES

Danny Williams of Sebastopol, California, wrote the following report on electro-magnetic fields and tachyon. The goal was to find out if extra-low frequency emissions affect fruit flies.

We have all heard the validated reports that describe the negative effects ELFs (extra-low frequencies) have on our health. Anyone who sits in front of a computer screen can feel the draining effects these devices have. Interestingly enough, for every report that proves our health is being affected by ELFs there's another report that refutes such claims. The EPA, in a preliminary report, said that ELFs "are a probable human carcinogen." Why aren't people more concerned? Because corporate America could never admit to the problem without being sued by every man and woman who developed cancer while working in front of a computer. So the best we can do is try and find a way to protect ourselves from the ELFs. The best way is to move into a house without AC electricity, somewhere in the unspoiled mountains. This of course is not practical. So I decided to do a study on the effects ELFs have on our friend the fruit fly. It is my intention to verify the effects and seek a solution.

Fruit flies have been vital to the study and understanding of genetics. Under the right conditions, only eight to ten days are required for an egg to develop into a mature adult. This allows for many generations to be studied in a relatively short period of time.

Imagine yourself as a scientist trying to discover the validity of different companies claiming to be able to protect us from the harmful effects of EMF (electromagnetic fields) or more specifically the effects of ELFs. What better way to study them than with fruit flies? They reproduce quickly and quickly display genetic defects when their environment becomes toxic. "FlyLab" is a biological experiment geared toward the study of ELF's effect on fruit flies.

Fruit fly facts

Size: The adult flies are very small insects, about 1/8 inch long (3mm).

Color: Body color is usually tan. The thorax is tan and the abdomen is gray underneath and black on top.

Description: Fruit flies are weak fliers. A feathery bristle is on the antenna. A distinguishing feature is their red eyes.

Habitat: With the end of summer season, many homeowners often encounter fruit flies in and about their kitchens and near garbage storage areas. They are generally found hovering around decaying vegetation and overripe fruit.

Life cycle: Female fruit flies lay their eggs on the surface of rotting fruit. These eggs hatch into larvae, which molt twice before becoming full-grown. Fruit fly larvae feed on the yeast organisms and fungi growing in the fruit and vegetable materials, and through their feeding efforts they soon turn their food into a semi-liquid mess. When the full-grown larvae are ready to pupate, they leave the rotten fruit for drier areas, usually to the sides of a garbage can. The time required to complete one life cycle is mainly dependent on the temperature of the growth medium and surrounding air. At sixty-four degrees, eighteen to twenty days are required for growth from the egg stage to adult, while at seventy-seven degrees only eight to ten days are required to complete the stages of development.

Control study: I acquired the fruit flies from a reputable organic fruit dealer and set up an open-air screen-covered test site. The temperature was regulated with a heating pad placed under the test unit. I maintained temperatures between seventy-two and eighty degrees. The larvae used in the control were grown on an organic peach. I continued introducing organic pesticide-free fruit every ten days. The study showed an increasing density in the fly population by the thirteenth day. I continued to observe normal propagation for an additional forty-seven days, making the entire control study sixty days long.

I then set up two different test sites, using the same size and material test fixtures and maintaining a constant temperature between seventy-two and eighty degrees. Using the adult population from our test group, I introduced fertile peaches and adults into both sites. In order to truly test the effects of EMF on fly population and propagation, I introduced a common VDT (cathode ray tube). Each site received identical VDTs, which were placed less than an inch away from the screen. The VDTs were then turned on and left on, broadcasting a strong EMF verified with a Gauss meter.

Dr. Cousens is an expert in ELF testing. Because he has tested dozens of devices and his integrity is impeccable, I chose to test the product that he reports as being the best tool available: Tachyonized Silica Disks (from Advanced Tachyon Technologies in Santa Rosa, California), which are simple to use, inexpensive, and 100 percent effective. Dr. Cousens does not have any monetary involvement with the manufacturer, but does supply Tachyonized products to many of his clients.

I flipped a coin to decide which site would receive the disks. I felt that by testing both sites against the control study, I could verify if there were any effect from the ELF of the VDT, and whether the Tachyonized Disks would have any beneficial effects. I named the sites Alpha and Beta and installed the disks in the Beta test site. The disks were installed over the circuit breakers of the entire Beta facility. At this point I failed to see the connection between these silvery four-inch disks hanging in the fuse box and the VDT some eighty feet away.

Alpha study (non-tachyon-mediated computer terminal screen)

The fruit flies seemed to propagate normally for the first three generations. About day thirty-six I noticed many new adults appearing with deformities, and the population was smaller. In the next two sets of new adults I saw even fewer normal flies and a drastically reduced population. By day fifty-two the entire experiment ended. All the flies had either stopped propagating or mutated past propagation. My conclusion was that the effects of the ELFs caused the mutations and subsequent demise of the population. This data supports a report by Kaiser Permanente that claimed pregnant women who spent more than six hours per day in front of a computer screen had twice the frequency of miscarriages. Listed below are some of the deformities observed.

Short-winged flies

These flies had such short wings they could not fly. I believe this is due to some defect in their vestigial gene, on the second chromosome.

Curly-winged flies

A couple of the flies seemed to have curled-up wings. This is believed to be the result of the curly gene, which is on the second chromosome.

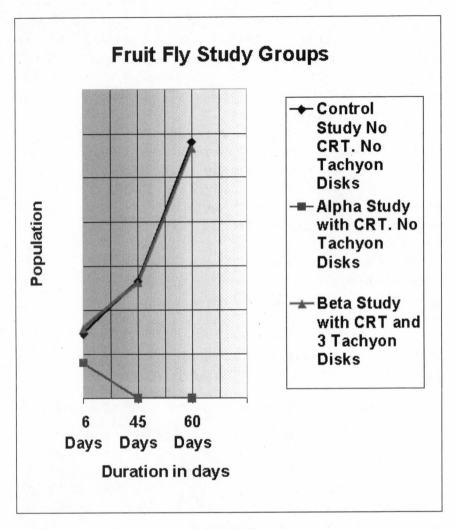

Fruit Fly Study Groups

Legend:

→ Control Study No CRT. No Tachyon Disks

■ Alpha Study with CRT. No Tachyon Disks

▲ Beta Study with CRT and 3 Tachyon Disks

Population

6 Days   45 Days   60 Days

Duration in days

Yellowish flies

Several of the new adults seemed to be much more yellow than the rest of the population. It is believed that these flies have a defect in their yellow gene, which is on the X chromosome. Because the yellow gene is needed to produce a fly's normal black pigment, these mutant flies should not be able to reproduce this pigment.

White-eyed flies

One fly was noted with white eyes. This indicates there is a defect in the white gene, which normally produces the red pigment in the eyes.

Beta study (tachyon-mediated computer terminal screen)

This study was uneventful. There were no mutations and no visible signs of any lack of propagation. By the end of the sixty days the population was at least equal to that of the study group in which no computer terminal screens were anywhere near their habitat.

This FlyLab study took over five months to complete. The results are quite obvious and enlightening. ELFs from our computer monitor in the Alpha experiments with no tachyon mediation proved deadly! Simply put, fruit flies cannot survive in a strong ELF field. The only difference in the Beta test was the introduction of Tachyonized Silica Disks mounted in the breaker panel of the building site. The results of the Beta test lead me to believe that the use of Tachyonized materials can protect us and our loved ones.

HUMANS AND EMFs

William Bennett, environmental consultant for New World Institute in Santa Cruz, California, wrote the following report on Tachyonized Silica Disk performance on humans.

The effect of EMFs on six people was measured using biofield analysis both with and without the Tachyonized Silica Disk installed in their homes. The fields were changed from being strongly degenerative to neutral or slightly regenerative for all seven people with one disk installed. Three disks were installed in three houses and tested slightly better than one disk.

Biofield analysis is a testing method developed at the Institute, where it was discovered that the size of the energy field of a person varies according to how beneficial anything he or she is exposed to (or is thinking about) is to him or her. The testing procedure is to measure the size of the subject's Biofield using L-rods, and then start asking the subject questions about how beneficial the device is for him or her. If whatever is being tested is not beneficial, the field shrinks varying amounts depending on how detrimental it is. If the field stays its normal size, the device being tested is helpful in maintaining a person at his or her current state of health. If the field expands beyond normal (over 100 percent) it has been found to be (usually) regenerative to the person in some way. This method has been used and taught at the New World Institute for eight years.

Results

Six people were tested to see what effect the electromagnetic fields of their homes were having on their health. Their biofields shrank to 15 percent to 30 percent of normal, indicating that the fields were very degenerative (see the graph below). I then installed a Tachyonized Silica Disk on the inside of the door of the circuit breaker box (in Joanne's case I put it next to the main cable coming into the house) and measured the fields again. They increased to 100 percent or more in all cases, indicating that the electromagnetic fields were not a problem anymore in all cases and slightly regenerative in some.

Biofield analysis indicates that the Tachyonized Silica Disk eliminates the detrimental effect of electromagnetic fields on humans. Use of one disk is sufficient for an average house. Six years of experience with similar devices indicates that it is not necessary to cover all of the circuit breakers with disks. The tachyon field around the disk drops off rapidly, so it would be better to emphasize placing the disk as close to the main wires coming into the house as possible rather than attempting to cover the breakers. Installing them on the door of the circuit breaker panel places them farther away than other installation possibilities, although it obviously worked in this test. The Tachyonized Silica Disk is an effective device to completely eliminate the detrimental effects of electrical devices.

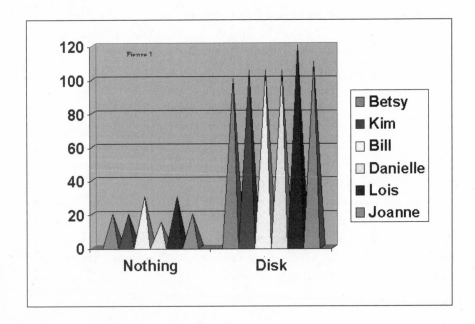

MICE

Carl D. Troppy, licensed natural health educator and owner of the Troppy Home for developmentally disabled deaf adults, wrote the following 1993 report on mice and ELFs.

The purpose of these experiments was to systematically track the effects of ELFs on a biological system and to determine what effects (if any) an SD-1 (a product provided by Advanced Tachyon Technologies) has on the ELFs created by a VDT (video display terminal).

As an independent researcher I take great pride in mapping out and executing what I believe to be objective evaluations. I chose to use feeder mice for these experiments for many reasons. Feeder mice have a very short life expectancy. Since they are bred to be pet food, they are normally sold and consumed within two to six weeks of age. I want to be clear that I am an animal activist and these mice were treated exceptionally well. At no time were they ever mistreated or neglected. To my way of thinking, selecting feeder mice first of all removed them from the food chain and secondly guaranteed them a much higher quality of life, one which could not have been experienced otherwise. Their lives consisted of high-quality food, clean water, exercise equipment, and adequate ventilation.

Since mice are not social creatures, I chose to evaluate three individuals, rather than groups. I set up three systems consisting of a typical cage providing adequate room, glass-type feeder dish, water bottle, and an exercise wheel. I chose to evaluate three individuals obtained from the same breeder. All three were from the same brood. Mouse #1 was named Rudy and was set up as a control experiment. Mouse #2 was named Bert and was set up exactly the same as Rudy except that I introduced a VDT, which was turned on and left on for the duration of the experiment. The cage is a rectangle and the VDT was positioned on one end. Mouse #3 was named Lucky and was set up exactly the same as Bert, including the VDT. This third experiment had to be conducted in another of my facilities, because Advanced Tachyon Technologies claimed that installing the SD-1 disks would have an effect on the AC current when they were installed on the breaker box. I followed the exact directions provided by Advanced Tachyon regarding the installation of three SD-1 disks, covering all the breakers at the entrance box of the AC electricity.

Rudy lived five months and five days from the purchase date. He was observed to be always active and generally interested in commotion in and around his cage. He always ate well and exercised.

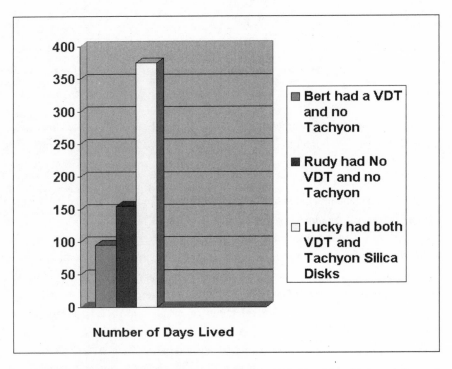

Number of Days Lived

Legend:
- Bert had a VDT and no Tachyon
- Rudy had No VDT and no Tachyon
- Lucky had both VDT and Tachyon Silica Disks

Bert, in the cage exposed to the unprotected VDT, lived for three months and four days. After about forty-five days, Bert seemed very nervous and was always extremely difficult to catch prior to cage cleaning. He did not eat or drink as much as Lucky or Rudy. When he died he had a full bowl of food and water.

Lucky, in the cage with the Tachyonized disk-mediated VDT, amazed me. Lucky, like Rudy, remained active from day one. He was not nervous like Bert. He ate as well as Rudy and was always interested in things going on around him. Lucky died after twelve months and ten days, which was approximately twice as long as Rudy.

From the beginning I maintained an objective approach and gave each experiment my full attention. I kept good records, recording food and water usage. I was skeptical that placing three disks onto the breaker box would have any effects, but experience and experiments proved otherwise. I have clearly demonstrated that the VDT did have a probable effect in shortening the life of one subject. Yet when the subject was protected, I found the EMFs actually seemed to have a positive effect, at least in this experiment.

A side note regarding the effects of EMFs: I was interested in finding out if I could feel any difference with the SD-1 installed on the breaker box, so I set up

Lucky in the same building as my office. It took less than one week for me to begin noticing that I was not fatigued after sitting in front of my computer for several hours. I am truly amazed. I don't pretend to completely understand how or why these Tachyonized SD-1s work, but all the evidence I have collected in my research over the past year definitely proves they eliminate the negative effects of ELFs.

As a researcher in the field of human potential, I feel the Tachyonized Silica Disks are a solution for the EMF problem that plagues almost everyone in this modern era.

MICE AND EMFs REVISITED

The following report was written by Sheryl Burton, a health care provider and independent researcher for over seventeen years.

After a complete review of Carl Troppy's experiments I was skeptical, so I decided to duplicate his research. My objective was to provide a second independent study of EMFs and mice by duplicating as closely as possible the Troppy experiment and then evaluating the results.

The testing results of the Troppy report indicated that ELFs were responsible for a considerably shorter life span of test mice. The conclusions of this report provided measurable test data that suggested a substantial problem and a potential solution.

Two new cages, substantially larger than the ones used in the Troppy experiments, were acquired. These larger cages were selected in order to increase the mice population. Ceramic feeding bowls and glass water bottles were installed as well as exercise wheels. Separate facilities were selected in order to test the effectiveness of the Tachyonized Silica Disks. Special care was taken to provide equal environments, including temperature and airflow and natural light. Then twelve juvenile mice were purchased for each site.

In both sites a common CRT was placed against the cage, turned on, and left on twenty-four hours per day. I continued this procedure for the entire duration of the experiment.

At Site 2 I installed two Tachyonized Silica Disks in the breaker box of the facility with the logo facing the circuit breakers.

Within the first fifteen days, the antisocial behavior of the mice became a problem. The cute playfulness of the juveniles became more and more violent.

My observation suggested that Site 1, which did not have disks, seemed to have a lot more fights and general irritation of the population. By day thirty, Site 1 had lost four mice and Site 2 had lost three. I immediately searched out an independent expert breeder who told me that the dominant mice would always harass the weaker until the strongest is the only one left. With this new insight I modified the testing procedure: I chose the two strongest mice from each site, and by dividing the cage provided the two mice with their own individual living space. I let the remaining mice loose in a field. I made this decision for the health and well-being of all the mice in the experiment.

My observations of Site 1 were alarming. Once the subjects were isolated they became much calmer and seemed to fall into a nice routine. Both mice tore up their papers and built sleeping spots in the far corner of their area. Both appeared interested in what was going on around their cage—at first. Then I noticed they became less friendly. They seemed more irritable and quickly startled. On day seventy-nine one of the mice went to sleep and never woke. The second mouse went to sleep on day ninety-one and never woke. Food consumption was consistent for the duration of their lives and neither had had any abnormalities or obvious health problems.

Site 2 was set up identically to Site 1. The only difference was the Tachyonized Disks, which I had installed in the breaker box. Both mice were very calm and curious. One of the mice built his nest close to the end of the cage. The other built it under the little ramp that went to the second level of the cage. It was obvious that neither of the subjects cared about the CRT, in contrast to the mice in Site 1, where both subjects seemed to try to stay away from the CRT. The mice in Site 2 appeared to exercise more. After the mice in Site 1 died, I found myself expecting the same results at Site 2. The fifth month of the experiment passed. I began to get a little excited that these disks just might work. After the ninth month passed and both subjects were doing fine, I installed Tachyonized Disks in my own home. After eleven months passed, I was telling all my friends, relatives, and business associates. Finally, day 375 came and it was clear that I had duplicated the original test data provided by Troppy. I had proved by duplication that the Tachyonized Disks are effective at protecting mice from the negative effects of EMFs. So in a heartfelt ritual, I took the two fuzzy subjects to a wonderful little wooded area next to a large field and let them go.

In my professional opinion as a health care practitioner and researcher, Tachyonized Silica Disks absolutely protected the mice from the effects of EMFs.

I was surprised at the effects EMFs have. I feel gratitude that a tool exists with the potential of protecting humans from the harmful effects of EMFs. Furthermore, it also appears that the disks enhanced the biological function of the mice, increasing the life span of our test subjects. I am, therefore, strongly recommending that anyone who watches TV or works on a computer quickly protect themselves. The results I encountered should be grounds for further research and studies to help illuminate the problems associated with EMFs and the solution created by Tachyonized Silica Disks.

SUMMARY OF LIVE-ORGANISM RESEARCH

The two mice studies, the fruit fly study, and the human research study by William Bennett all show that ELFs disrupt the function and health of living organisms. The mice research showed that the mice exposed to ELFs had one half the life span of the control mice. The fruit fly research showed an increased mutation rate and the end of the ability of the fruit flies to propagate after five generations. In the human study, there was a decrease in the energy fields up to 85 percent with an average decrease of up to 78 percent.

The theorized reason for the detrimental effects of ELF fields is that they are not coherent. Their lack of electrical coherency, we postulate, is what has the detrimental effect on the electrical system of all biological systems.

Tachyon makes the incoherent electrical fields of the ELFs coherent again. It does this by rebalancing and re-energizing the SOEFs of the electrons and their current flow. This explanation is consistent with and reinforces our point that tachyon reorganizes and energizes the SOEFs of everything that exists in the material world, from electrons and electrical current to plants, animals and humans.

These four studies show that tachyon protects us from the effects of ELFs. Whether it is a video terminal, TV, electric juicer, or hair dryer, the field made coherent by tachyon seems to even enhance cellular electrical integrity and health.

In these studies there is an additional finding that suggests that when the electrical fields we are exposed to become coherent, they have a beneficial effect on all living organisms. We postulate the reason for this is that since all living cells have an electromagnetic field, the coherent electrical field brings these living cells into a higher order of organized coherency and therefore functionality.

The other great advantage of unified fields created by tachyon energy is their direct application on the body. In regular waking consciousness the brain is usually in a state in which one of the two brain hemispheres dominates. We either function rationally (left-brain hemisphere) or intuitively (right-brain hemisphere). A state of balance is very difficult to attain. This "normal" state corresponds to an EEG of thirteen to thirty Hz and is called beta-state. This beta-state is characteristic of the fragmented, disharmonious consciousness of most people.

When the brain is in the beta-state, the energy connected with the heart chakra and the physical heart is disharmonious. The heart energy possesses twelve different vibrational aspects that are incoherent when the brain is in a state of disharmony. In this state the connection of the energies of the heart and the brain with the magnetic field of the Earth is disrupted.

If we manage to bring the entire energetic field of the body into a unified field via tachyon energy, we will attain a harmonious, coherent energy pattern of the heart chakra. Reaching such a state influences the brain and engenders a balance between the two brain hemispheres. The brain frequency then reaches the alpha-state (7.85–13 Hz). In this state, the brain is more receptive and creative. This is also the state in which the so-called super-learning occurs. In this way, the heart reaches a harmonious energetic state in which its innate love is more easily perceptible. Thus, the energies of the heart and the brain more easily entrain with the magnetic field of the Earth. This enhances an increased awareness of our connection to the Earth. Our entire system becomes energized and balanced.

The frequency of the Earth, and thus the frequency of a balanced brain and heart, is usually assumed to be 7.83 Hz. However, newer findings indicate that the Earth's vibration is already shifting and has even fluctuated to 9.2 Hz. A coherent energy field of a person would therefore also correspond to 9.2 Hz; the person would be connected and entrained with the energy of the Earth. Tachyon energy can help maintain a person's energy field as the pulse of the planet continues to evolve. This is extremely important if we are to stay balanced during the Earth's changes. Naturally, we can best benefit from these enormous possibilities attainable through tachyon energy when we adopt a harmonious, conscious lifestyle. As an integral part of such a lifestyle, tachyon energy can be of invaluable help in reaching a state of profound harmony with all life, including ourselves.

CHAPTER 7

THE HISTORY OF MODERN TACHYON RESEARCH

The use of invisible tachyon energies was known to highly sophisticated ancient cultures. For example, ancient Hebrew priests wore flax linen because they knew it drew in energy. We now know that flax is a natural energy antenna. In the modern era, however, the rediscovery of non visible energies and its astonishing potential began with the revolutionary inventions of Nikola Tesla (1856–1943).

For many years, Tesla had worked on a method for utilizing an invisible energy source as an alternative to alternating-current generators, which were a previous invention of his. His sponsor, George Westinghouse, feared suffering substantial financial losses from this new invention and took drastic steps to prevent Tesla's success. Finally, Tesla parted from Westinghouse and continued his efforts on his own, only to have these efforts destroyed by those with little vision and consciousness.

In the summer of 1931, Nikola Tesla, along with his nephew, Peter Soro, conducted successful and well-documented tests with an engine that powered an automobile with no visible energy source. They used a Pierce Arrow, which was a heavy and luxurious motor vehicle at that time. Using his "energy converter" and no fuel, the car reached speeds up to eighty miles per hour. Tesla had reached his goal—almost. The technology worked.

So as early as the 1930s problems resulting from the use of fossil fuels might have been solved. Several months after Tesla's invention was completed, however, the Pierce Arrow automobile company went out of business. Influential men who feared losing money because of Tesla's new invention almost certainly were responsible for this unfortunate development. Tesla was thus forever deprived of the opportunity to present his technology to the public.

Tesla's converter was probably the first free energy device of the modern era. His converter transformed an unseen energy into the usable frequencies of electrical energy. It is possible that tachyon served as the connective element in this technology. Tesla's converter could be used to power automobiles of all types, as well as function as a power supply for buildings and industrial complexes.

Another pioneer in free energy research has been Dr. T. Henry Moray from Salt Lake City. Moray succeeded in developing a converter for such energy that weighed only twenty-eight kilograms yet had a power capacity of fifty kilowatts. On July 13, 1931, Dr. Moray presented his invention to the American Patent Office, which confirmed that the machine functioned perfectly and generated fifty kilowatts with no visible energy source. But because the energy source was invisible and untraceable, Dr. Moray's application for a patent was denied. Like Nikola Tesla before him, Dr. Moray was stopped by ignorant political and economic circles that, in their shortsightedness, prevented a future without the use of fossil fuels and nuclear energy. Until his death in 1974, Dr. Moray shared his knowledge with small groups of interested scientists. As had been Tesla's fate, there were also attempts made on Dr. Moray's life. These threats understandably led him to become very cautious and restrained in presenting his invention.

From biographies of Nikola Tesla and Dr. Henry Moray, it becomes obvious that the global ecological and social problems resulting from the present technologies employed for generating energy could have been solved a long time ago. Technologies that could supply all people with energy already exist and have no harmful side effects. They are viable and there is no logical reason for delaying their use. Perhaps we still lack the maturity of consciousness that would enable the application of these technologies. It would be easy to put all the blame on ignorant politicians and greedy economic leaders. From a spiritual perspective, however, the people in power only mirror the society from which they emerge. A human society based on harmony and compassion would not produce such greedy and shortsighted leaders.

As wonderful as inventions of free energy converters may be, they are not the primary cures for the problems we are facing on a global level. A shift in global consciousness is needed for the clarity of purpose to create the deeper solutions and shifts needed for the healing of the planet. More than ever, a return to a state of harmony, balance, and healing is called for, individually as well as globally. Once this transformational process is completed, the utilization of alternative life-supporting technologies will be a logical consequence.

What we therefore need are not new machines for generating energy (the inventions of Tesla and Dr. Moray would fully suffice), but ways to support spiritual awakening and healing for ourselves and the planet. Because Tachyonized materials enhance our access to the state of perfect health and harmony, as it is contained in zero-point energy, tachyon tools are full of very promising potential for helping us achieve that global shift in consciousness.

THE TACHYON ERA HAS BEGUN

Since the inventions of Tesla and Dr. Moray, a plethora of research material pertaining to faster-than-light energy has been accumulated. As far back as the 1920s and 1930s, physicists such as Seretzov, Stanyukovicz, and Sluneiderov have postulated the existence of energy moving faster than the speed of light that could be converted into usable energy.

In 1966 Gerald Feinberg and George Sudershan, working independently of one another, defined faster-than-light energy as Tachyons. The word "tachyon" is derived from the Greek root for "high velocity." Tachyons are subatomic particles moving faster than the speed of light. Other notable scientists sharing this view include Professor Shinishi Seike, director of the Japanese gravitation-research laboratory; Todeschini, from Italy; Pages, from France; Kooy, from Holland; and Wyniatt, from New Zealand. They all share the opinion that tachyon energy offers a rich reservoir of usable energy.

Dr. Hans Nieper of Hannover, Germany, is one of America's best-known physicians in the fields of cancerous disease, multiple sclerosis, mineral and electrolyte metabolism, aging, and the prevention of cardiac infraction. In 1953 Dr. Nieper theorized the existence of faster than light energy. His theories were confirmed by numerous measurements of NASA satellites between 1967 and 1971. Dr. Nieper, in his book *Revolution in Technology, Medicine and Society,* claims that the existence of tachyon energy has been proven beyond doubt since 1975 and that it will revolutionize the world. He articulates both the Hanover, Germany, and Toronto, Canada, symposiums illuminating the speakers and the inventions which harness tachyon energy. His vision predicted a day when science would harness tachyon for the benefit of the body, mind, and spirit.

The problem is no longer proving the existence of tachyon energy—it is in harnessing the energy and turning it into usable electrical energy. Many distinguished scientists have worked in this field with mixed results. What these scientists were and still are trying to accomplish is the conversion of tachyon energy into usable electrical energy.

There is one exception to this. An American scientist of German descent named David Wagner, co-author of this book. Wagner had a different vision of the benefits of tachyon energy. His vision was a clear realization that the conversion of tachyon energy into usable electrical energy would in fact not solve this planet's growing crisis because it is not a crisis of energy, it is a crisis in consciousness. Wagner recognized that everything evolves out of the tachyon field. The only thing that was missing was a concrete, practical method that would allow the infinite potential of tachyon to be harnessed to benefit life on Earth in a way that could elevate consciousness.

Today, such a method exists. It has been the life's work of David Wagner, whose inventions include the Tachyonization™ process and the Quality of One™ seminar. This work has been changing the way hundreds of thousands of people look at and experience life. Despite all obstacles, the tachyon era has begun. We give thanks and acknowledgment to the various scientists who have provided the foundation for this new era and have thus paved the way for a tachyon revolution.

Always the inventor, by age five David had already developed quite a reputation for disassembling anything electrical in order to understand it. His first invention came when he disassembled the family's toaster. Clipping the coils on one side, Wagner laid the toaster on its side and placed buttered bread into it. He then activated the toaster so that the bread would be toasted only from the bottom. This gave him fully melted butter that oozed into the hardening bottom of the toasted bread. Today we call such a device a toaster oven. From that first successful creative moment forward, Wagner never stopped inventing or experimenting.

WAGNER AND THE SCIENCE EXPERIMENT

Wagner often brought humor and a sense of the prankster into his inventions. In the third grade, he built his first electrical generator for a science fair. It was a hand-crank unit capable of lighting three 100-watt light bulbs. As a boy, Wagner was fascinated by the conversion of magnetic energy into electrical energy. He recounts that he was observing how energy traveling through the wires would actually move beyond the insulation to a higher capacitance or ground. Seeing the energy swirling around the wires and leaking onto his hand as he held the wire, Wagner didn't understand why he couldn't feel the minuscule quantity of leaking energy. Furthermore, he could not understand the fact that nobody he knew could see the energy swirling around the wire.

Frustrated by this fact, Wagner began to formulate a new experiment he hoped would help enlighten his teacher and classmates. He postulated that if an electrical current running through one channel could be passed to a large capacitor with a high storage capability and then discharged to a solid ground, perhaps someone might be able to see or feel the energy flow. Using his teacher as an unsuspecting guinea pig, he set off to prove his theory.

Placing the generator on a table directly in front of his teacher's desk, Wagner disconnected two of the three light bulbs by unscrewing them from the generator's output sockets. He then tapped the hot side of the generator and ran a wire to the metal seat bottom of his teacher's chair, securing the exposed end of the wire with black electrical tape. Realizing that he needed a large ground potential to complete the circuit, he ran a wire from the ground of this generator and routed it to the teacher's metal stapler. Wagner's theory was that if he used his teacher as the capacitor, then she would finally feel what he was talking about and maybe the class would see the energy flowing. The young Wagner studied the potential outcome of the experiment and became unsure about the end result. Not being exactly clear about what was going to happen, at the last minute—when his teacher came back into the room and sat in the chair at her desk—he developed an alternate plan.

It occurred to Wagner that he should ask the class bully to help him by explaining that he wasn't strong enough to light all three light bulbs, and he wondered if the bully could crank the generator fast enough to light all three bulbs. Well, the bully quickly jumped at the challenge not knowing that two of the three bulbs had been unscrewed. He waited until the bully had the single light bulb lit as bright as it could possibly be. At this point Wagner could see the energy flowing out of almost every pore of his teacher's large body, which was acting as a capacitor. He was surprised that she couldn't feel the energy, and none of his classmates seemed to be able to see this incredible sight. Perplexed, Wagner quickly grabbed a stack of papers for the final phase of his experiment. He approached his teacher and sweetly asked her to staple his papers.

The experiment went just as Wagner predicted. The energy stored in his teacher's body was released through her hand as she made contact with the metal stapler. In fact, her body did act as a large capacitor, storing an enormous amount of energy which was released through her arm, finding its way to the ground potential of the stapler. In a flash, his teacher did in fact feel the energy. Wagner's theory had been validated. As the electricity from the generator surged through his teacher, she began screaming at the top of her lungs.

As the teacher shrieked—her hair sticking straight up—Wagner realized that in an odd way the second part of this theory had been demonstrated. His classmates could see the result of the energy flow. The bully, who was still cranking the generator, gave way to a tremendous belly laugh that drew the teacher's attention straight to his fist cranking away on the generator. He didn't know that he was producing the electrical energy she was experiencing, but he sure found her screams and hair standing on end very funny. The teacher immediately presumed that this event was his doing, and she began bellowing at him to get out of her classroom. She demanded that he go directly to the principal's office. As they both headed for the office, everyone could hear her loudly berating the bully.

Wagner was astonished by the chain reaction, and at the same time, he realized that maybe he overdid it just a little. He quickly disassembled the wires and firmly screwed the other two light bulbs into the sockets. One of the office staff came into the room and announced that the teacher was OK, but she was in the nurse's office and would not be returning to class that day. Wagner was both relieved and concerned. Wagner played hooky for the next two days as his family moved into another school district.

His skills assured his success in all walks of life. Eventually he found himself working for a Fortune 500 company as the head of Quality Assurance. One day, during morning meditation, he received an insight: "Today, something will happen that will change your life forever! Remember, it is for the best." He was twenty-eight years old, and ecstatic at the prospect of discovering a way for people to remain vertical, or perhaps some other intriguing new discovery such as his faster-than-light energy machine or a better way of dealing with EMFs. He shared that morning's prospect with one of his spiritual engineering peers. Later that day, he helped move a heavy filing cabinet with the vice president of the company. The cabinet fell on him, crushing him and rupturing three of his spinal disks. Moments later, a crew of people lifted it off of him as he lay there in agonizing pain. But he had to laugh when his engineering friend asked, "Is this it?" In fact, David realized, this was it.

David had ruptured three lower lumbar disks verified by an MRI study. His disability was so severe that 14 orthopedic surgeons could not find a way to help. One eventually convinced David to have surgery. During surgery the surgeon damaged the nerves that ran down David's left leg. The worst that could happen did. David now had to cope with a new unbearable level of pain. A new MRI study was ordered and the results sealed David's future. While living with incredible pain and enduring many hardships that came with it, David was eventually found to be totally and permanently disabled and began to receive social security. Through the years David tried everything: crystals, hands-on healing, magnets, meditation, Reiki therapy, chiropractors, pharmaceutical drugs, royalight jacket, cortisone, and the famous surgery. Nothing had worked. Nothing relieved the pain that kept him from walking more than fifteen minutes, sitting for more than twenty, driving, picking up his baby, or even holding his wife. Life was a struggle to find positions that didn't cause too much pain.

Then finally one day, while in a state of deep meditation, David questioned his very existence and reviewed his life, searching for that "remember this is for the best" insight. Only then did the true revelation of the future evolve within David's being. He immediately envisioned the entire process that would restructure natural materials at a submolecular level in order to conduct tachyon energy. Was this the answer? This was indeed the answer, and the process became known as Tachyonization™. Materials that are Tachyonized are instrumental in holistic healing and spiritual awakening. Once the first Tachyon machine was completed, David began experimenting with the first Tachyonized materials. By placing these materials over the injured area of his lower back, he began to feel and experience the healing effects of tachyon. Throughout the next four months, he found the pain in his back to be continually diminishing. After six months of constant use, Wagner began to realize the potential his invention held for the world.

For more than a year, he tested his products on more than a thousand people, and in 1991 made his discoveries public with the formation of Advanced Tachyon Technologies. His work presently focuses on the conversion of tachyon energy into usable energy for healing biological systems. This breakthrough has inspired a revolution that is changing the way the world looks at energetic medicine.

HOW DOES TACHYONIZATION WORK?

The Tachyonization process is 100 percent patentable. Wagner spent many months deliberating the benefits and expenses of enforcing a U.S. and European patent. His decision has been not to patent the system but rather to keep the process proprietary, an action that he speculates has saved millions in patent infringement lawsuits and has assisted in keeping prices for the materials as low as possible.

The Tachyonization process revolves around the restructuring of certain materials at the submolecular level. Wagner's Tachyonization machine opens up a window or exogate into the point of singularity or oneness that exists just prior to frequency. This window is the gateway between our frequency world and the non-frequency world of faster-than-the-speed-of-light energy where everything exists in a state of pure potential. At this point of singularity, anything that is in the "space" is altered at the submolecular level, causing its natural molecular structure to realign in such a way that it becomes a permanent antenna for the non-frequency Tachyon energy. Once a material has been Tachyonized, the rich flow of tachyon energy through the material will maintain the molecular alignment of the material permanently. The material will still look like the original host material, yet now it is a permanent tachyon-energy antenna. Just as a radio antenna would never need to be sent back to Sony to get new music, these Tachyonized materials never need to be sent back to be re-Tachyonized. Once the fourteen-day process is complete, the Tachyonized materials are permanent antennas that will serve for many generations.

Restructuring materials is a common process. For example, if we were to take a piece of steel and strike it over and over again with a large hammer, we would be exciting the molecules with every blow. As the molecules of the steel excite into a larger orbit they wildly move about. As they begin to slow, they naturally begin to align themselves to the north and south poles of the planet's magnetic field. When we are done, we see we still have a simple piece of steel, yet further testing of the steel reveals that we have created a permanent magnet. Of course, in no way are we suggesting we hit the Tachyonized materials with a hammer. This example is used only to demonstrate that restructuring materials is not that difficult. Since the status of the invention is proprietary, we cannot divulge the details of the Tachyonization process. We can, however, mention what it is not. The Tachyonization process *is not a frequency, spin manipulation, or transfer*. It *is not a high frequency or coil technology.* It *does not use sound.* It *does not use sacred geometry to inform products.* It is *not a photon-based technology.* It *is not an SE-5 or other forms of radionics-based technology.* It does not require *prayer or meditation.* The technology *does not use crystals or orgon technologies.* It *is absolutely not operator-sensitive.*

Many people are renaming their old frequency technologies, oftentimes in an effort to exploit the public, by calling their frequency-oriented technologies "Tachyon." One such company illegally used Wagner's trademarks and offered a rotating magnet box for sale to the general public as a "Tachyonized machine." Problem was, it worked only with magnetic frequencies. The outcome was tested and quickly dismissed by independent researchers.

We truly hope to witness the continual spiral of order/chaos/order to bring integrity and understanding to the world. Tachyon energy is the source of all frequencies. Tachyon energy in its purest form is a gift, a revolutionary breakthrough that is changing the world. It is a scientific breakthrough in a technology that has seen some of the world's most distinguished scientific minds evolving and speculating upon its potential. David has met with physicists from many countries, some of whom have been working for many, many years to restructure materials at the submolecular level in an attempt to create permanent tachyon antennas.

Until 1993, Wagner had to oversee every Tachyonization run. In late 1993, he completed another invention, the Dynamic Wave Processor, (DWP). The DWP monitors each machine throughout the process, 24 hours a day. Any deviation from the optimal operating parameters causes the DWP to immediately shut down the affected machine, canceling the entire Tachyonization process for that machine. It then issues a report pinpointing the probable failed component. This guarantees that every single run is 100% successful. Today the Tachyonization procedure has evolved into a technology that anyone can run. This has allowed Wagner to train highly qualified personnel to maintain the equipment as he expands production at a rate that has almost kept up to the demand. Today the technology is virtually limitless it its expandability and potential.

In essence, this means there has been a historical breakthrough in which we can now harvest tachyon energy. Tachyonized materials can be used for the healing and transformation of consciousness on the planet. This breakthrough creates the preconditions for us to directly experience a new paradigm in holistic healing.

DNA STUDY

The following graphs illustrate the neg-entropic effect of Tachyonized water on DNA in the research done by Dr. Glen Rein, a well-known biophysicist. It has been shown that DNA rapidly degenerates when taken out of its intracellular home in the nucleus. Dr. Rein has investigated many different frequency generating devices as well as Tachyonized material in an effort to ascertain their ability to keep the DNA from degenerating when taken out of the cell nucleus.

His preliminary studies revealed that the Tachyonized materials were the only technology that had a neg-entropic effect on the DNA integrity.

This research was done with a Hewlett Packard UV absorption spectrophotometer. The study measured the effects of different frequency devices and Tachyonized materials on preventing the degeneration of the DNA. Results which show a compression or reqinding of the DNA signify a neg-entropic effect or the prevention of degeneration.

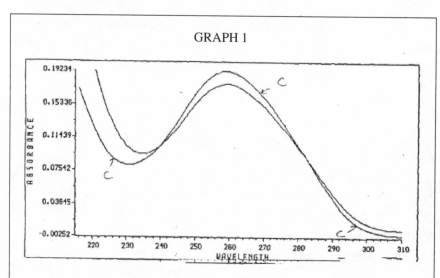

GRAPH 1

This graph shows how the Tachyonized water reversed the entropy of the disintegrating DNA. The proof in this conclusion is that the Tachyonized sample is physically longer and has a higher amplitude than the control. The increased length of the tachyon treated DNA indicates the DNA is rewinding, which indicates a reversal of the degeneration of the DNA.
This reversal is also referred to as neg-entropy.

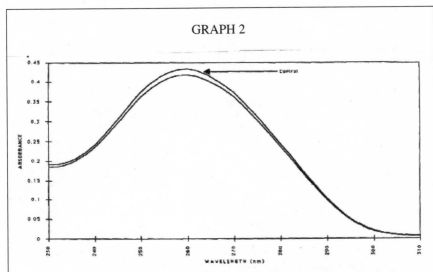

GRAPH 2

This graph shows DNA treated with a particular frequency generating device.
The treated DNA is shorter and has less amplitude than the control, indicating that
the frequency had a degenerating (entropic) effect on the DNA, or did not prevent
the DNA from degeneration.

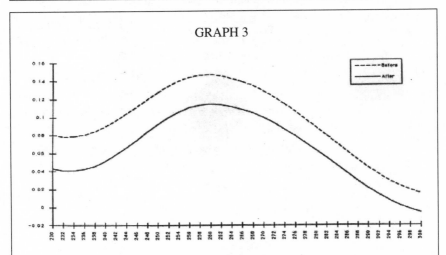

GRAPH 3

This graph shows DNA treated with a particular frequency generating device
which is different from the frequency generating devices of Graph 2.
It is shorter and has less amplitude than the control. This means it is more
degenerated (has more entropy) than the control.

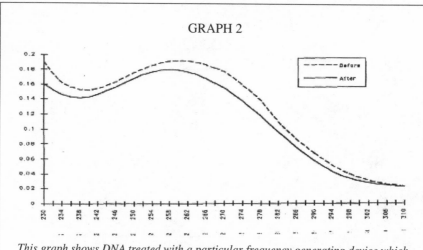

GRAPH 2

This graph shows DNA treated with a particular frequency generating device which is different from the frequency generating devices of Graphs 2 and 3. It is shorter and has less amplitude t han the control. This means it is more degenerated (has more entropy) than the control.

The implications for human health and longevity are quite exciting. Some of the hottest research today in anti-aging is connected with telomere degeneration and consequent DNA unraveling in the intracellular nucleus. Telomeres are like the end-caps of both ends of the DNA and appear to unravel with age.

Researchers are theorizing that if we can figure out how to stop telomere degeneration at the DNA poles we can stop the aging process. The research by Dr. Glen Rein with Tachyonized materials may be one of the ways to stop the telomere degeneration, DNA unraveling, and consequently, the aging process. From the Tachyon holistic theory point of view, what we are again seeing is that the Tachyonized materials (by energizing the SOEFs of the DNA) are maintaining the integrity of the telomere and obviously the DNA.

TYPES OF TACHYONIZED MATERIALS

A thorough understanding of the different types of tachyon antennas brings clarity to the many potential uses of Tachyonized materials for enhancing health on all levels.

Five basic types of Tachyonized materials and avenues for focalizing tachyon energy are now being used:

silica glass cells;

silica disks;

natural fabrics;

liquids; and

organ-specific foods, herbs, and nutrients.

Each of these different avenues produces a slightly different intensity in terms of their clinical use.

We tested many different forms of silica and natural materials in an effort to identify the best media in terms of cost and effectiveness. After several years of research it became clear that industrially produced glass meets all our needs. High-quality silica glass has a number of benefits: it Tachyonizes wonderfully, it is readily available, it does not deplete our planetary grid of natural quartz crystal, and it is inexpensive.

Through the Tachyonization process, research has proven that we can cause the molecular structure of silica to align in such a way that the silica glass lens becomes a focal directional point that can then be placed on different points of the body like a laser. The outcome has proven to be very effective for healing, especially pain relief. This has been demonstrated throughout the world. Natural healing through the neg-entropic characteristics of Tachyonized materials is becoming an acceptable alternative in holistic health care. The available research materials and reports strongly demonstrate its healing abilities. However, more is not necessarily better. The right focalization of tachyon energy to the specific area is all that is needed. One of the most exciting discoveries accompanying the invention of the Tachyonization machine is that the materials altered can be used on virtually any part of the body. This led to widespread research as we began to develop more specific antennas. In the case of pain, it was found that when the antenna was applied, most pain issues were resolved. Through thousands of treatments it became clear that Tachyonized materials provide the body with everything needed to heal itself.

All we had to do was to affix a tachyon antenna directly to the area we wanted to target. The glass cells in the different sizes and shapes have their specific healing effects on the body because of their ability to energize and reorganize any localized disrupted SOEFs.

Silica disks, according to our research, are one of the most powerful and most highly focused tachyon antennas available to the general public. The Tachyonized silica discs offer the largest surface area and intensity of all the hard silica materials. For this reason extensive research was done in the area of electromagnetic fields. Manmade EMFs are diffuse and chaotic fields, which have been postulated to cause cancer along with a whole host of other health problems. We discovered that the silica discs, when properly applied, were able to neutralize the unhealthy effects of EMFs by turning the normally diffused AC fields into balanced coherent fields. Tachyonized silica discs not only reorganized the chaos of electricity, but these reorganized AC fields actually showed regenerative properties when applied to biological systems. So, Tachyonized silica discs actually resolve one of our modern problems. In fact, our research shows Tachyonized silica discs to be 100% effective. This is a monumental breakthrough because the "vampire" effects of manmade EMFs bombard almost every human in our modern society.

The rebalancing effects of the SOEFs inspired the initiation of new research projects. Another area of particular interest is cellular phones. Through a joint venture with Japan and Germany, a tachyon antenna was developed that creates coherent patterns that actually negate the negative effects of the cell phone. A small Tachyonized cell, attached to the outside of the cell phone, actually protects the user. ELFs, AC electrical currents, and cellular phones all operate under vastly different conditions and are composed of different frequencies. They can all become coherent and orderly when subjected to a focused tachyon energy field. With this understanding, the possibilities of how this energy can help restore balance to our world are truly limitless.

As the research unfolded it was discovered that not only were we able to Tachyonize silica materials, but there appeared to be many natural materials that could be Tachyonized into focusing lenses. The Tachyonized liquids are primarily water and liquid silica. Silica is essential to all living things and has been labeled one of nature's building blocks. Tachyonized silica molecules enhance the body's natural ability to increase water absorption of essential proteins, acting as a binding agent. By binding exiting calcium, protein, and water molecules together, they strengthen and revitalize the skin, hair, and nails and aid in the remineralization of the bones. Tachyonized silica is absorbed into all areas where silica is stored in the body such as the bones, connective tissue, and the lungs. Research shows that Tachyonized water has a significant effect on the blood within thirty minutes of being taken sublingually.

Our earliest research centered on pure water that was Tachyonized (see Coyle research, following). Because water passes through the blood-brain barrier, it was easy to see and feel the results. Studies demonstrated that the whole body benefited from the Tachyonized water. The water slowly converts the whole body into an enhanced tachyon antenna. The process works so well for liquids, it has been extended to include massage oils, creams, and lotions with positive success.

The following report was written by Michael Coyle and Christine Baillie, and was performed in 1992 using an SE-5 Biofield Spectrum Analyzer.

Summary of Report: Testing was conducted to determine both the positive and negative energetic effects displayed by two products. Evian water, a well-known product, was tested in order to provide a control by which to contrast the other product—TW-4 Tachyonized water (distributed by Advanced Tachyon Technologies). Both products were found to be excellent-quality waters with high bioenergetic potentials, with all negative effects falling well within acceptable parameters.

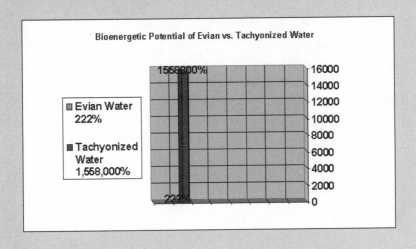

Results

Test Conducted	Sample Source	Signal
	Evian	222%
	TW-4 Tachyonized Water	1,558,000%

Explanation of Terms and Measurement Scales

Bioenergetic (or biofield) measurements represent resonance signals that exist in the subtle, subatomic fields of energy. These energy fields structure the formation of matter.

"Signal amplitude" indicates the strength of the signal being generated by the sample being tested. The "bioenergetic potential" category would have to be above 85 percent to be acceptable. All others would be required to fall below the 10 percent range to be deemed acceptable.

PSI Research is an independent testing laboratory. One of the primary endeavors of PSI Research is to utilize subtle energy analysis technology and methodology in the area of evaluating products and technologies that may exhibit high bioenergetic potentialities, in order that these may be made available to the general public for the betterment and advancement of mankind.

Two other natural materials that Tachyonize well are silk and cotton. Due to the interlocking of the individual fibers, these materials become true omni-directional antennas. This discovery led to a multitude of research in healing with soft, comfortable fibers. Inevitably, an aero fiber was discovered that actually cross-weaves silica strands into a pliable material. Out of all the soft products, the aero fiber material proved to be most beneficial when covering larger parts of the body. Studies have shown that due to the omni-directional field of tachyon energy, the Tachyonized aero fiber affects both the physical and emotional bodies.

THE ADVANCED TACHYON TECHNOLOGIES PRODUCTS

The following report was independently conducted by Dr. Norman McVea, Ph.D., Director of Research for the Oxygen Research Institute, an independent facility. The Institute was hired by Advanced Tachyon Technologies to research their Tachyonized products. Neither Dr. McVea nor the Institute is a distributor for these products, nor do they have any financial interest in these products or in the Tachyon Health Center. The work with these products was completed over a ninety-day period using a number of test subjects and a variety of methods to substantiate the precise effects of these Tachyonized products on physical, mental, and spiritual health. All the testing was done at the Institute's independent research facility and the findings are based on an in-depth familiarity with these products established during testing.

Tachyonized shoe insoles

This is the best insole or shoe insert tested yet. A few years ago the Oxygen Research Institute tested a high-quality magnetic acupressure insole from Japan, which I was very impressed with. However, Tachyonized shoe insoles far surpassed these in effectiveness.

One test subject was able to play tennis on concrete for the first time without suffering foot pain. All the test subjects reported that stress was reduced during walking and jogging, especially on hard surfaces. The insoles appeared to have an immediately soothing and relaxing effect and there appeared to be an increase in circulation. It is an excellent tool for people who have any foot problems or for those who stand on concrete or who are on their feet all day.

Tachyonized sheets

Numerous test subjects were placed in the Tachyonized sheets. Each person spent a minimum of fifteen minutes in the sheets; most spent about one hour. Every subject reported an experience of deep relaxation, and some even went into a deep sleep (all trials were done during the day). Psychological tension disappeared, even on the most stressful subject. Some subjects listened to music or spiritual talks. The subjects' intuitive abilities were greatly enhanced—they experienced the meaning of the lectures with greater understanding and clarity. Overall, every test subject that used the sheets was able to enter into a meditative state quite easily. It seemed to increase the alpha brainwaves.

It was not unusual for subjects to report various spiritual phenomena such as out-of-body experiences and an increase in such psychic abilities as clairvoyance. A number of test subjects experienced a reduction of aches and pains. A subject with arthritis experienced less stiffness in her lower back.

A therapist/test subject used it during his work with patients. He found it to be very helpful during their sessions and found that patients made better use of their therapy time.

Some subjects received massages and bodywork while lying on the sheets. Their bodies seemed to open up, allowing for deeper work to take place, amplifying the massage's result.

The sheets were also placed on driver's-side car seats. Subjects reported a reduction in tension and fatigue and an increase in alertness. There was also less wear and tear during long-distance driving. (Before recommending it for driving, however, I suggest further in-depth testing to be sure that some individuals wouldn't become too relaxed, compromising driving safety.)

A test subject used it while writing long hours with the computer. He felt it definitely enhanced his creativity, reduced computer-related stress, and even reduced typing errors!

Tachyonized cells

Tachyonized cells were placed in headbands, and test subjects reported that they were very effective when used for stress reduction. When the cells were placed inside cloth belts, test subjects reported some reduction in back pain. When the cells were placed over the eyes, the subjects reported a relaxation in the eyes. All applications brought some improvement.

A headband comprised of three Tachyonized cells was used very effectively as a meditation tool.

Tachyonized water

This water product seems to raise vitality while detoxifying the body. Some users reported an enhanced sense of well-being and heightened perceptions. One subject decided to take a larger quantity of the Tachyonized water than recommended. She had found a smaller amount successful and decided if some is good, more is better. Unfortunately, this was not the case. She experienced a too-rapid detoxification response—slight nausea, headache, and general malaise.

Tachyonized scarf

Most of our test subjects could feel the Tachyonized scarf; however, a few could not. This product seems to bring a psychological lift to the wearer as well as an energetic stimulation to the throat area.

Most of my research concentrated on Tachyonized sheets and shoe insoles. The test subjects and staff enjoyed the sheets, as they delivered the highest amount of tachyon energy and lent themselves to various applications.

We tried to objectively measure the energy from these unusual products. Traditional biofeedback instrumentation was unable to accurately measure the energy produced by these Tachyonized products, as it was much too refined and subtle. Although the results were through interviews, the responses were consistently favorable for all tachyon treatments.

We measured the general vitality rate of each of these products with the SE-5, a subtle energy/radionic-measuring device. Almost all of the test subjects realized a noteworthy increase in their general vitality when using the products on a daily basis. Overall, I consider Tachyonized products to be of tremendous value as tools for stress reduction, meditation, creative visualization, consciousness, rejuvenation, and psychic exploration. They are truly user-friendly mental health appliances.

Once again, the testing results indicate that Tachyonized materials have a broad effect on biological systems. In this particular study, Dr. McVea found the Tachyonized materials to be of "tremendous value as tools for stress reduction, meditation, creative visualization, consciousness, rejuvenation, and psychic exploration." The reason for this is when the SOEFs are energized with the tachyon antennas, the entire body-mind complex experiences subtle shifts back to balance and begins to operate at a higher level of order.

By employing advanced kinesiology, the field strength of various Tachyonized antennas can be measured. The Tachyonized silica disc has a fifteen-foot field. The aero fiber material has a nine-foot field, silks have a nine-foot field, and cottons have a six-foot field. The largest antenna tested is made out of the aero fiber and works like a mattress pad that bathes the entire system in tachyon energy.

Exciting new possibilities now arise in the area of certain herbs, vitamins, minerals and other substances. It is a revolutionary breakthrough in our ability to transform glands, organs, tissues, and bones in our body into tachyon antennas. What this means is that when a specific body part is transformed into a tachyon antenna, it draws tachyon energy to it. Because of this, its SOEFs are energized and restructured. We are now able to do tachyon healing treatments on the inner organs, taking holistic medicine to a new level of healing and rejuvenation. Tachyonized substances are drawn to specific areas of body, so if they are Tachyonized (changed at the submolecular level) when they become incorporated into the biological structure they turn it into a tachyon antenna. This energizes and enhances the specific function of that structure.

For example, research with Dr. Cousens has shown that the algae from Klamath Lake, *Aphanizomenon floaquae* (AFA), specifically activates the hypothalamus and certain parts of the pituitary. Blue-green algae is the only vegetarian substance Dr. Cousens has been able to find that actually activates, heals, and rebuilds the hypothalamus (the master organ in terms of regulating and affecting the whole endocrine system). Tachyonizing the blue-green algae causes it to be an antenna for the tachyon energy, which is carried right up to the hypothalamus and pituitary gland. The elements of the Tachyonized blue-green algae are absorbed into those structures and turn the hypothalamus and pituitary into specific tachyon antennas.

Once the Tachyonized material reaches a specific location in the body it creates a neg-entropic effect. This means the Tachyonized material organizes the subtle organizing energy fields of those particular biological structures (in this

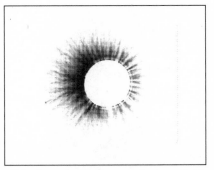

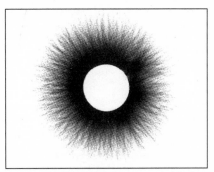

This photo shows the normal energy field of non-Tachyonized Klamath Lake Blue-Green Algae.

This photo shows the energy field of Tachyonized Blue-Green Algae.

case the hypothalamus and pituitary) so that they may start moving toward their optimal function. This creates youthing.

Another example of a Tachyonized biological material is vitamin C. Tachyonized vitamin C would tend to go to the adrenals as well as to connective tissue. The adrenals have the highest concentration of vitamin C in the body. When the Tachyonized vitamin C goes to the adrenals, it becomes incorporated in the structure of the organ, thereby changing the adrenals into a specific tachyon antenna that will draw energy to balance, energize, and move the adrenals toward health.

Clinical findings show that when biological materials are Tachyonized, about half as much of the biological material is needed to have the same optimal effect. This seems to be the case with Klamath Lake algae and melatonin. Tachyonized melatonin that activates the pineal is about one tenth to one twentieth of the dosage people normally need for sleep effect. We now have and are continuing to develop organ- and gland-specific Tachyonized biological materials. These are being developed to utilize this new carrier delivery system.

CHARGING SUBSTANCES USING TACHYONIZED MATERIALS

There is a huge difference between charging something with Tachyonized materials and actually Tachyonizing that material. Certain companies have emerged that have acquired Tachyonized silica materials and use them to charge the SOEFs of their products, believing that they have Tachyonized their products. They then market their product, claiming it to be a tachyon antenna. Of course, this is not

121

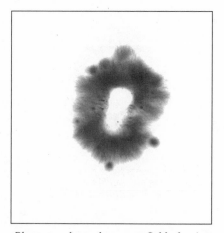

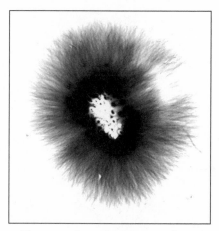

Photo one shows the energy field of a ripe strawberry prior to charging the SOEFs with Tachyon energy.

Photo two shows the same strawberry, after the SOEFs were charged using the Tachyonized Silica Disk for 20 minutes.

possible. Tachyon energy is faster than light, and for this reason it does not work with gravity. You cannot make Tachyon energy stick to anything. The truth of the matter is still very exciting: if you place something inside of a tachyon energy field, the neg-entropy will in fact allow the item to become very coherent and energized. With coherency comes an increase in vitality as the subtle organizing energy fields become energized and organized. In the simple case of a strawberry, we can actually see the charging effects. In the photos above, a strawberry has been photographed using Kirlian photography.

Note that in the second photo there is a much more defined and expansive energy pattern. It is in fact the same strawberry, but it has been "charged" using Tachyonized silica discs. When this strawberry is eaten it will provide the body with a much higher source of "strawberry energy," not tachyon energy. As the body uses the strawberry as a building block, it is incorporating the wonderfully high energy of the strawberry. Another way to see the difference is with a carrier-specific source such as Klamath Lake blue-green algae. When the algae is charged and then eaten, the pituitary and hypothalamus use the algae as building blocks, incorporating the highest energy potential from the algae. What happens when we actually Tachyonize the algae is different. When the algae is Tachyonized through the fourteen-day process, it is changed at the submolecular level and becomes a tachyon antenna. When this antenna is eaten it is absorbed by the target organ and becomes part of it. This new part continues to be a tachyon antenna and thus continues to charge the target with the neg-entropic effects of tachyon. This is a key to the healing and therefore the youthing process.

Research also shows that Tachyonized materials provide a stepping stone into the energetic continuum. The key is when the submolecular change happens in the Tachyonization process and the material goes into a particular organ, it acts as an antenna for tachyon. Because you have regular cell metabolism and new cell growth, the tachyon-activated organ doesn't stay permanently Tachyonized; you must keep taking the Tachyonized material to maintain the organ-specific tachyon antenna. Charging algae is also very good, but it cannot do what the Tachyonized algae does. This creates a whole new meaning to "super food" and opens the door to the potential of restoring health and vitality.

OTHER AREAS OF
TACHYONIZED MATERIAL USE

Tachyon energy works wonderfully with agricultural endeavors. In the United States and Germany there are test results that demonstrate that plants react just as well as humans when grown in a rich tachyon energy field. When specific soil condiments are Tachyonized, the seedling begins to grow in a soil that is highly bioenergetic. This creates stronger and larger growing plants, and of course plants with a higher vibration and energy. This in turn provides a higher-energy fruit. As we consume the fruit, the life force of the fruit becomes ours, increasing our energy vibration. The potential for increasing the vitality of our food source on an individual and global scale is exciting.

There have also been excellent results with pets. Many veterinarians incorporate Tachyon tools in their therapies. The stories of pet youthing seem endless. Also, work is being done to increase the bioenergetic value of water. David developed a simple design that was presented to the government-authorized bottling company for India. India's water is among the poorest in the world. The design actually provides water to the bottles that is between eight and ten times more bioenergetic. This simple design could be incorporated into most water bottling plants rendering superior water. The list of possibilities is endless.

We can identify five major areas of Tachyon healing application. The first is for the restoration of health and balance on the physical, mental, emotional, and spiritual levels. The second is for human health, maintenance, and rejuvenation. The third is for the enhancement of strength and stamina in sports. The fourth is for enhancing communion with the divine. And the fifth area is the restoration and healing of the planet. The question is not what, but how do we incorporate tachyon energy's neg-entropic effects into our less-than-balanced worlds.

SUMMARY

Tachyonized materials that bring the tachyon energy into the human organism and to our material life have tremendous therapeutic and self-healing potential. The Tachyonized materials that have been developed have been able to effectively eliminate the negative effects of AC currents as they go through electric blankets, juicers, blenders, televisions, and computers. When the Tachyonized silica discs cover all the breakers in the electrical breaker box, the entire house is protected, so one only needs a few discs for the whole house. People are able to use the Tachyonized glass cells to achieve tremendous relief of pain in their body, or they may wear a Tachyonized cloth over larger parts of the body on a 24-hour basis, once again providing tremendous relief from chronic pain and energizing the system. Tachyonized carriers, like vitamin C, Klamath Lake algae, and melatonin, are able to directly influence the health of targeted organs or glands.

There are tremendous clinical as well as preventive implications for Tachyonized materials. Therapists throughout the world and particularly in the United States and Europe have been using Tachyonized materials with great success since 1992. Not only does it work well for humans, but it seems to activate and heal all life forms on the planet. The success stories are truly amazing and consistent. We stand on the brink of a whole new era of health care, which includes linking us up to the entire energetic continuum. Opening the flow of the energetic continuum creates not only physical healing, it also helps rebalance, energize, and heal our spiritual existence. Blockages in all these areas have the potential to be dissolved. Then, as the energy continually flows through the use of a Tachyonized antenna, strength and stamina are increased. Mental blocks clear and concentration is enhanced. As the energetic continuum becomes free-flowing, our natural urge to evolve strengthens, as does the natural pull towards meditation, prayer, and the increased desire to enhance our communion with the divine.

HEALING BEYOND ALL CONCEPTS

Healing physical diseases is of course a wonderful, desirable thing. However, we try not to focus on just the visible physical results. The healing of our entire being and the expansion of our awareness is our ultimate goal. Sometimes this may mean that a physical disease is not healed, but that instead the healing of the soul is completed. To reconnect with the sweet inner peace of our soul is the greatest healing of all.

On the path toward this goal we often experience physical healing. The healing of physical symptoms, however, is not in every case necessary for the inner growth of a person. Tachyonized materials don't force physical healing but rather help us find our true self as a whole being.

TACHYONIZED MATERIALS IN COMBINATION WITH OTHER THERAPIES

Tachyonized tools have been found to be extremely beneficial when combined with other therapies, particularly vibrational therapies. Tachyonized materials should not, however, be used with radiation therapy or chemotherapy because as the body is affected by these therapies, the tachyon energy would try to neutralize the negative effect. If radiation or chemotherapy is part of your treatment plan, it is best to complete that first. Afterward, Tachyonized materials can be used to help recover from those treatments.

When Tachyonized materials are used in conjunction with frequency therapies, the practitioner finds that the Tachyonized materials balance out the treatment, and if the Tachyonized materials are continuously worn, they substantially shorten the healing time expected. This insight is explained by the tachyon-SOEF-frequency understanding of our paradigm. When the frequency therapist pushes the body or system in or out of balance and then applies Tachyonized materials, the SOEFs convert the tachyon into the needed frequency to either continue the healing process or rebalance an area that may have become unbalanced by the exposure duration or incorrect frequency of the application. Tachyonized materials have therefore become the secret tool of tens of thousands who use them as an adjunct to their healing practice.

We have trained health professionals from A to Z. The list of qualified therapies using tachyon is extremely long, but we'd like to include some of it here to give readers a sense of the scope of professions that benefit from it.

Professions That Use Tachyonized Materials:

Alexander Technique practitioners

Aromatologists

Art therapists

Ayurvedic physicians

Biofeedback analysts

Cellular repatterning practitioners

Chiropractors

Color therapists

Craniosacral therapists

Dance movement therapists

Dentists

Dowsers

Energy workers

Feldenkrais Method therapists

Feng shui masters

Flotation therapists

Foot reflexologists

Hellerwork practitioners

Herbalists

Holographic alchemists

Homeopathic and naturopathic
  doctors

Hypnotherapists

Iridologists

Jin shin jyutsu practitioners

Kirlian photography practitioners

Light acupuncturists

Light therapists

Magnetic therapists

Massage therapists

Medical doctors

Nurses

Nutritional therapists

Oliver Technique therapists

Osteopaths

Oxygen therapists

Pediatricians

Physical therapists

Plastic surgeons
Polarity therapists
Pulse diagnosticians
Qigong masters
Rapid Eye technologists
Rebirthers
Reiki practitioners
Relaxation and breathing teachers
Rolfers

Shamans
Therapeutic Touch practitioners
Toning and music therapists
Touch for Health practitioners
Tragerwork practitioners
Veterinarians
Vibrational healing therapists
Visualization teachers

APPENDIX

TESTIMONIALS

The following testimonials are included to give readers a feeling for the depth of healing power that tachyon has given to people.

"I used to be a professional soccer player in the major league. Both my knees are covered with scars from my many operations. I always have pain while jogging. While in Munich, I was introduced to Tachyonized products. After using the Tachyonized silk pad for fifteen minutes, for the first time in a long while I had no pain while running that night. I am experienced in working with crystal therapy, and I was amazed at the enormous power of tachyon energy. In the future I will combine both methods."

"As a rather devout light worker and meditator I can say in all honesty that these tachyon products are profoundly and supremely empowering. It feels like that which we call Shakti. My life has been energized and illuminated considerably. Hats off to Mr. Wagner. These are magnificent products!"

"In March 1993 I started using Tachyonized products in my practice. I have seen them have an incredible rejuvenating effect on my clients."

―――

"Dear Tachyon friends,

Since the use of Tachyonized materials I have experienced an increase in energy and alertness, increased spirituality with all that is, and genuine love and concern for all loving things. It helped my grandmother's back pain, aunt's arthritis, and my friend's carpal tunnel was healed. I just love it. Thanks to you all for making them available."

―――

"When I received my first tachyon products, I decided to use them on my family since I was familiar with their medical history and could monitor their responses fairly easily.

My sixty-five-year-old mother has suffered with carpal tunnel syndrome for several years. She has not had a peaceful night's rest in years. She would complain of waking in the early morning hours with her hands aching and numb. After applying Panther Juice [a Tachyonized B vitamin solution used for alleviating pain, trauma, bruises, sprains, and sore muscles], I taped three 8mm cells on her wrists and had her wear wristbands for three days and nights. She applied the Panther Juice three times a day and wore the cells and wristbands faithfully. I also started her on Tachyonized water three times daily. She has not had a sleepless night since using the Tachyonized products. She wears her wristbands to work, around the house, and to do her canning and preserving. The best news of all is that she no longer complains of any pain in her hands.

My brother had knee surgery for a torn ligament about a month before I received my first tachyon shipment. He had been on crutches and was having a problem regaining the elasticity in his knee. Since he works as a derrickman in the oil fields, on drilling rigs, it was essential that he have full movement for his own safety. Before he used any Tachyonized products he could only bend his knee at a ninety-degree angle. After using Panther Juice and a Tachyonized Sports Wrap for a day he could bend his knee so that his heel could touch his buttocks."

Joyce M.

―――

"Eight weeks ago I sprained my ankle, sustaining a severe injury including swelling, ecchymosis (bruising) and pain, incapacitating me from bearing weight on that ankle. An orthopedic surgeon who examined my foot suggested I have x-rays taken because of the amount of bruising present, which led him to believe I had fractured my ankle. The x-rays were negative. This type of injury would ordinarily take at least two to four weeks to completely and comfortably bear weight on, let alone run on. After two weeks of using Tachyonized cells and a Tachyon sports wrap, the swelling was completely gone and I was able to hop up and down on the previously injured ankle—totally pain free!"

Christine Cummings, M.D.

Kaiser Permanente

"A little over a year ago, I was having a terrible time with tennis elbow. I couldn't even lift up a coffee cup because it was so painful. I tried a lot of different things including wearing a copper bracelet. None of these remedies worked. I overheard a salesperson telling someone of the Tachyonized Massage Oil and asked her about it. She asked me to rub some of it on the troubled area. Instantly I felt a warm feeling and decided to buy some. As I said, that was a little over a year ago. I have not had any problems with tennis elbow since. My husband is a real skeptic, but he also had tennis elbow so I let him try some of the Tachyonized Oil. I am very pleased to say that he no longer is bothered with the pain.

About six months ago I had surgery and decided to try the oil on the scar from the surgery. The scars are minimal and the relief I have received from using this oil is unbelievable.

I do massaging and have now decided to use your oil, although it is more expensive, as I notice a big difference when I use the regular massage oil. Because of the expense, I used to just use the Tachyonized Oil only on the problem spots but have changed to using the Tachyonized Oil all the time. The results are much better and my customers are very pleased. I can't explain the difference in oils other than it is Tachyonized.

You have a great product and I'm so glad I happened to be at the right place at the right time the day I found out about your product."

"Just wanted to let you know that these are the most effective tools I have tried yet to balance and energize myself! I am over eight months pregnant and was suffering from a chronic lower back pain of one month's duration when I ordered your 15mm cells and taped two on my lower back. Within twenty-four hours, my back pain disappeared completely. Not only that, but my Braxton-Hicks contractions of my uterus are much less painful as well! Needless to say, I have recommended your products to my family and friends and have ordered a bunch more cells for other parts of my body! I am currently using the necklace and wristbands, and have so much more energy now. What a Godsend! Thank you!!"

———

"I am writing to thank you for the months of June, July, and August—and hopefully the rest of my life.

After living with cluster headaches for over thirty years, part of my life is now missing—the HEADACHES! I haven't had a headache since my Tachyon treatments in late May. Having been on one prescription pain medication or another since 1976 (and living on Excedrin prior to that), it still seems strange to feel so good! However, I'm having a wonderful time adjusting to it!

I have only one question regarding Tachyon—is Tachyon another word for MIRACLE?"

———

"To Mr. David Wagner,

David, my friend, it gives me great pleasure to sit and share with you my Tachyon journey as of late and since meeting you nearly two years ago.

I gotta tell ya right up front Mr. David, nothing's been the same since, nothing. We are both aware of the wonderful benefits and user-friendliness of your Tachyon products. I find it quite ironic, David, that when the vibration of humanity seems at times so chaotic I can remain so calm and focused. A coincidence, I think not. As you well know David, my profession is just a little out of the norm. I can tell you with complete confidence that Tachyon's energy truly enhances my awareness, concentration, and ability to perform under seemingly impossible circumstances and conditions. I have yet to share Tachyon with a motorcycling friend who doesn't rave of its benefits. Although trying to get a written testimonial from them has yet to be a reality, I'm working on it."

———

"David,

The pain I once accepted as the daily norm, I no longer live with. I live with my Flexcell twenty-four hours a day. As I have been using the Tachyonized skin products, I have noticed an incredible smoothness come about my face, neck, and arms. The quality of my sleep, I can promise, has been enhanced by the introduction of my silk pillow and a stout dose of Tachyonized water before laying my body down. Not to mention my Happy Souls that allow me to remain on my feet for hours on end with virtually no pain in my feet, legs, or lower back. This was not possible B.T. (Before Tachyon). The warm glow from within at times cannot be described, but is so visible in the radiant flow we bring from others. I pray from the core of my being that humanity will soon come to understand this simplest of concepts. As we radiate, they perceive. In turn they radiate, all the while unaware of what it is they are actually perceiving, yet without fail, the glow shines forth. You know what I'm talking about, David. This angelic enhancing— Godsend of a wonder—we have come to know and love. We see Tachyon at work every single day of our lives. The smiles we receive from the faces of others are nothing more than the mirror image of our inner self. What more can we ask for. Of all the times we have chosen to be, this surely is the best of all. To think, David, so good as it seems now and we're just getting started. The future is looking oh-so-bright thanks to the beautiful light you have brought to the Planet. As we accelerate into this new dimension, please remember this always. We have come to this planet for no other reason but to help others as much as we possibly can and to polish our own inner beings to the brightest radiance, all the while spreading happiness, love, and harmony wherever we may go. Remember this little speck of Beautiful Light that Burns within Me has been touched by God, through you, David Wagner.

It is for this that I share with you David, my innermost experiences. We are both aware of times when words are better left unspoken. This happens to be one of those times, David. So close your eyes for a few minutes and we'll connect, communicate, and radiate.

I thank you so very much David for your love and support. May love, light, and happiness be forever a glow from within."

"Dear Mr. Wagner:

After visits to the office of three medical doctors, three surgeons, two chiropractors, one neurologist, two physical therapists, and one religious practitioner—and with no relief from the chronic pain which inhibited my left shoulder—I found your clinic. At that time, I was taking (four times a day) pain-relieving anti-inflammatory medications that caused stomach problems. At night I took two Vicodin and a sleeping pill to get to sleep. And even with that, I would awaken every three to four hours in pain.

My energy level was very low. I was not functioning at work, nor could I function in any other area of my life. I received threats of termination from my employer due to my work not being up to par because I had so much pain in my left shoulder. I looked and felt bad all of the time.

Before I found out about your clinic, I was ready to give up. I came to your introductory meeting and was impressed with what I saw and heard. So I decided to give your treatment a try. Mr. Wagner, that was the best thing I could have done for myself. Within twenty minutes, the pain was completely gone. For the first time in one and a half years, I was able to sleep all night. I woke up expecting to be in pain, but I was not. I'm not sure how the Tachyon process works, or what it does exactly, but I do know that it works well. I returned for one more treatment, which completed the process.

I stopped taking all of the above medication the same day of the first treatment, and now, two and a half months later, I still have no need for the pills. I feel good!!! My energy has returned.

I really appreciate you and the treatment that has returned my life and health to me. I highly endorse this treatment."

———

"Dear Tachyon Health Center:

I had extreme lower-back and leg pain when I came in for my first Tachyon treatment last week. It was hard for me to sit down or get up. It hurt to walk any distance.

Basically, I have lived with varying degrees of pain for the last twenty-eight years. It originated when I contracted spinal meningitis and was given eight spinal taps within two months. I heard about Tachyon Health Center and decided to try an alternative healing technique.

After my first treatment at your Center, the pain was 95 percent diminished within twenty-four hours. I was able to resume my natural activities (pain-free) the second day after my first Tachyon treatment. This is the first true relief I have experienced in twenty-eight years.

I'm not sure how Tachyon works—but it works! Thank you, very much."

———

"Dear David,

I would like to share with you my experience in using Tachyonized water and cells to improve my performance in fifty-mile bike races. For the past five years my husband and I have entered the Rosarito-Ensenada fifty-mile Fun Bike Race each year. It is called "fun" because of the twelve-mile hill in the middle of it. We spend all summer prior to the last weekend in September biking to get in shape for this event. We always try to beat our personal best, as a way to measure our physical condition. (And see if we're getting old yet!) We are fifty and fifty-one years old, and stay in good condition, since we ski patrol during the winter. This year Tom, my husband, had biked about 1600 miles during the summer, many more than my measly 500. It showed when we biked together, as his stamina and speed were much better. The week before The Race, we did a practice fifty-miler. I had been taking large doses of Tachyonized water for about a week (twenty drops two to four times a day). I was biking so fast that Tom finally asked me to slow down so we wouldn't wear ourselves out before the end of the race. I was usually out in front and frequently waited for him to catch up. As we pulled away from the stop-lights I would sprint ahead and get in behind the lead biker, usually a trim twenty-something guy. Once when I did this and found myself in the midst of a pack of them, one of the guys said, "You're a good biker!" For a twenty-something guy to say that to a fifty-something woman—well, that comment was a keeper! I was sure Tom was not feeling well because it was so unusual for me to be out in front. But he felt fine. Still, I wasn't sure I was going to give all the credit to the Tachyonized water. Let Rosarito be the true test. The prior year I had been slower than my personal best by about five minutes, and I had trouble with the heat and with breathing and Tom had to wait for me. At the end of the race I had felt nauseous for almost an hour. This year besides taking lots of T-water, I placed two T-15s over my lungs and two T-12s on my upper thighs. Somewhere in the middle of the Big Hill, I asked my husband if he wanted me to wait for him. Sweetheart that he is, he said no, for me to go for it and give it all I had. So I did. The end result was that I ended five minutes ahead of him, and he beat his personal best. I also beat my personal best by five minutes. The best part of all was that I felt GREAT! No nausea, no heat, no problems, just a tremendous amount of energy. I had to take the cells off my body quickly in order to calm myself down. This experience showed "skeptic me" beyond a shadow of a doubt that the Tachyonized products have a very powerful effect on my physical performance and level of energy. I have found them effective in other ways as well, to speed up healing of cuts and chronic sores, in meditations, foot soles in hiking boots, and face creams to reduce wrinkles. I am very pleased with the results of the face creams, but unfortunately I didn't do just half of my face or take a "before" shot, and I can't convince Tom yet to let me experiment on half of his face. However, by far the most dramatic results were in the Rosarito bike race, where we push ourselves to the limit each year to try and shave off a minute or two from our time and where I could see almost ten minutes' difference from the prior year! Great stuff! Thanks!"

———

"Dear Mr. Wagner:

Thank you! Thank you! Thank you! The Tachyon treatment worked. After years of encumbering pain, dead-end massage therapy, and costly chiropractic visits, I walked through your doors to find relief. My life and physical conditions have improved considerably since. I had spent eight years in pain following an accident and coped sporadically until a month ago when I endured three consecutive nights without sleep (due to an aching shoulder and constricted neck). I hired a private masseuse ($125 for two hours of therapy) while in Florida. The therapy had little effect. My partner John told me of your Tachyon method and I read the literature on the flight home. The next day we met for a forty-five-minute treatment session at which time I could feel notable results in my condition. At first, you may remember, I had trouble lying down and turning over on your table but within minutes I was agile with reduced pain!!! The ensuing thirty-minute treatment several days later led to an 85 percent improvement for my condition. Within a week I WAS CURED COMPLETELY! To this day (a month or so later) I have no pain, no sleepless nights, and complete agility. As a young man of twenty-six, I live with optimism of being an athlete once again and engaging in rugged activity without compromising movement. I wish there were a universal way of convincing people of this treatment. It has a dramatic effect that no medicine can rival. Plus there have been no side effects. I will gladly and publicly endorse this method if it can serve others as it has served me.

PS: My partner John is also doing well as a result of your Tachyon treatment."

———

"Dear Mr. Wagner:

I would like to share with others my experience with Tachyonized water and my cat. I made an appointment to have his teeth cleaned. The vet was alarmed at how thin he was (he had always been thin and a very finicky eater). He did a blood test and found his kidney in very bad shape and said it was probably what they call "kitty AIDS" and there was no hope. Devastated, I took him home, determined to save him. I immediately started him on vitamins and three droppers of Tachyonized water every morning and evening. In a matter of weeks he has gone from 5.5 pounds to 9.5 pounds, his fur is more beautiful than it has ever been, and he now tears around the house like a kitten (much to our joy). He sits in front of the refrigerator the second I get out of bed and meows loudly until I give him his special water. Words can't express my gratitude for saving Wheatie's life. Thank you."

"On March 13, 1996, I found a friend. It was on this date I was introduced to Tachyon. I am sixty-nine years old and I have rheumatoid arthritis. It had gotten so bad that I was in a wheelchair; I could not stand up. My arms and hands hurt so much that I could not use them. I started using the Tachyonized cell, taping it on my knee joints. I also massaged my legs with the Tachyonized oil. Within just a few days, the sore joints didn't hurt. If the pain comes back, I repeat the process wherever I need it. Every night and morning I rub my legs, shoulders, arms, and wrists with the massage oil or Panther Juice. I now sleep without pain. I am now walking with a walker, going up and down stairs, and doing my own cooking. I am not saying that Tachyon is a cure for arthritis, but it has made life much more comfortable."

"My research has demonstrated to me that the Tachyonized TLC bars [the most powerful Tachyon healing tool, reserved for trained practitioners] are the ultimate balancing instruments. Profound success occurs when using the TLC bars and the techniques learned in the Pain Management Workshop."

"Just a note to add to my earlier letter regarding your Tachyonized water, which I have been taking for a cartilage problem in my hip. In the course of events, I had a dental procedure that involved regenerating periodontal bone in order to do an implant. The doctor was pessimistic that the bone would come back. In three months the bone regenerated itself and was found to be nearly twice as dense as my normal bone in other areas of the mouth. This is specifically due to Tachyonized water. I could feel the process and the effect of the water most precisely. Extraordinary. The doctor was absolutely amazed! Thank you again."

"Muffie is my sixteen-year-old poodle mix who developed an inch-long growth under the skin over her ribcage. Six drops of Tachyonized water twice a day and the growth was reduced to half the size in two days and completely gone in four days and to this date has not returned. She is now a proud owner of two stretch headbands that are worn daily crossed over her heart that have improved a heart murmur from a four on a scale of six down to a three. And she enjoys an improved energy level as the result. Thanks, Tachyon!"

"I had a customer from southern California who has had arthritis for the past fifteen years. I rubbed the Panther Juice into her hands and she cried tears of joy. It was the first time in fifteen years that she had been pain-free. That evening she had a friend rub Panther Juice into her most painful area, her back. It was the first time in fifteen years that she had slept a full eight hours straight, free from the nagging pain that normally keeps her awake at night."

"I fell down a flight of stairs and sustained acute contusion of the right foot with damaged ligaments and hemorrhage in the tissues. The pain was quite extreme. I was taken to the hospital where the X rays showed no bone damage. I was told I would not be able to walk on it for a week and I was put on crutches and told I would need them for a week or more. The four-inch Tachyonized Sports Wrap came early the next morning via UPS. I immediately applied Panther Juice and wrapped my foot with the wrap, including seven T30-RO cells in the wrap. After twenty minutes, I had no pain, and in about ten hours I was walking without crutches as if the injury had never happened. Weeks later, I am still injury-free!"

"I have been confined to my house for four years because of a disabling accident that causes great pain while walking. Normally I can barely get off the couch, so even walking to the mailbox has been nearly impossible. I received my Panther Juice and rubbed it into my lower back area; within minutes I was able to walk around the house pain-free. I was so excited by this freedom I walked to the corner store and back to my house without experiencing any pain."

"We have been having very good results with the Tachyons. They definitely work on all kinds of pain. The most spectacular was a woman who had a hysterectomy. Two 75mm cells (in pouches) were put around her abdominal area and she never experienced any post-operative pain. Even her doctors were amazed.

"We had a teenager relieved of menstrual problems by wearing a 75mm cell at the focal point. We had a woman who was cold all of the time no longer cold after wearing a scarf. The scarves also relieve tension around the neck and shoulder area. I know that the scarf gives me a wonderful feeling of well-being when I am working at the store or am around people. I feel like it strengthens my energy field and protects me from other people's energies. I also had someone else tell me that she felt that way too when wearing her scarf.

"I had another woman tell me that after wearing her 75mm cell over her focal point for three nights, she did not need to wear her crystals anymore. A friend of mine who is very sensitive to energy felt the wrap from about eight feet away. Her back was facing me when I took it out and was opening it up. She swung around and said 'What is that?' I put it on her and in five minutes she said she was getting too hot and could not wear it anymore. She got her period the next day without problems or discomfort, but the best thing was that she hasn't been constipated since—which is going on three weeks now. Another sensitive that I know says that the tachyon energy is so strong that it could become illegal.

"Some of my friends in 'Brain Gym' are using Tachyonized cells whenever they have to hold points in the body—they are holding the cells over the points. I use them for 'cook's hiccups' and place cells on the two neuromuscular stress points on the forehead. These points are used in 'touch for health.' These are the techniques to balance the body's energy fields. I felt the energy very strong and felt the balance occur faster than usual."

———

"I am almost tired of being asked why I look so healthy now. I just answer by saying Tachyonized products gave me back my dog, who was close to euthanasia due to chronic arthritic pain; my seventy-eight-year-old mother, who has been fading away from multiple health problems and last but not least myself! I have so much energy now that other people can feel it across the room!"

———

"Tachyon is fabulous! I recently fractured my ankle. From past experiences of injuring the same ankle and using the wisdom of Western medicine, I expected them to cast and immobilize and then wait and wait (six to eight weeks), then go through physical therapy and still have an ankle that is weak. Instead, I decided to use alternative ways of healing my ankle. Thanks to the Tachyonized beads (that I taped on each side) my ankle is growing stronger by the day and it has only been two weeks. When I remove the beads to rest my foot/ankle, within twenty minutes, the entire foot starts to swell. I put the beads back on my ankle and the swelling goes away!

I highly recommend the beads for any injury—it speeds up the healing time and adds strength to the injured area."

———

"Our cockatiel's mate died two years ago. He has been completely quiet since then. A few weeks ago, I noticed that his eyes were stuck shut. Every morning, I got some warm water and a cloth and opened them up for him. Luckily I remembered our chakra balancing kit and placed the 24mm sapphire cell on his cage directly over his favorite perch. The next morning he woke us up singing! His eyes were opened wide! A few days later my wife still could not believe that the cell worked at all. She took it off. Wouldn't you know that his eyes were shut and running when I woke up the next morning, and he wouldn't make a sound. I quickly cleaned his eyes and returned the cell to its original place. Now his eyes are fine again and he sings often. Even if someone barely jiggles the front door knob, he makes noise like a watch bird!"

———

"In 1978 I was diagnosed with a precancerous condition, a thyroid nodule. Surgery was performed on the benign tumor, which was wrapped around my thyroid gland. I was left with about half of the gland. For the next eighteen years, I took three grains of synthetic thyroid every day. In 1992 I began using Tachyonized products extensively. I made it a point to wear a silk scarf over my scar as much as possible, and to rub the massage oil on my throat, as well as use Tachyonized water daily. Two years ago, I decided that the thyroid hormone was making me too nervous. On a lark, I began breaking them in half, cutting the dosage to 1.5 grains. In the beginning of 1998, I just did not want to take them anymore. I went and had my thyroid uptake done, and lo and behold, a perfectly normal amount of thyroid is now being produced!"

———

"In 1991 I began experiencing pain in my wrists. It was getting so acute that sometimes I would cry at night as I prayed for relief. I knew it was due to having a death grip on my camera for years, and I also knew I would never put my camera down. I was prepared for a life of pain. The discomfort was aggravated by typing and carrying anything in my hands. I started experimenting with Tachyonized cells. For one month I wore the 24mm cells over the tenderest areas of both my wrists. I protected the cells with the Tachyonized Wristbands. After about the third week, I couldn't believe that the sharp pains had subsided to a dull ache. After about five weeks, my wrists only hurt after a hard day of using them. At the end of the sixth week, I could flop my hands around without flinching. Now, I have absolutely no pain in my wrists, but when I travel or do hours of typing, I certainly wear the wristbands for maintenance."

"Dear David,

It has been few months since the October training in Stellshagen, or maybe a few light-years...

I am very glad that I decided in the last minute to participate despite not having worked my long exercises as I should have done. It is difficult to say, but yes, I am grateful that my first-grade pendant fell on the floor and broke.....It was a chance for a leap forward instead of staying on the same level.

Actually I just had an endoscopic exam done on my large intestine where I had had a (benign) tumor for the last 5-6 years. The doctor wanted to take out a few inches of intestine last September because of the risk the tumor could turn to cancer. Last July I negotiated with my doctor and told him I would bombard that tumor with tachyon energy and find out what it would decide to do. Further, we convened to postpone the surgery and do another endoscopic exam instead. It turned out that most of the tumor had healed off just leaving a scar, and the tiny rest had finally come out of the intestinal wall where it had been incrusted and could be taken away easily. Thus no more need for big surgery! I am very sure that my consistent work with all kind of Tachyonized tools (algae, water, silica gel, TLC bars, Flexcell etc) has greatly contributed to this healing process.

Hedwig"

"The insoles energize me during long hours of work and play. The wristbands healed a broken toe that I had been nursing for 5 weeks—and did it overnight! They also healed a sprained great toe overnight!
The Tachyonized products keep me balanced.

Isabelle H."

"Dear Mr. Wagner,

Now that I've used the Panther Juice for a couple of weeks I am writing to tell you how helpful it is. I've also been using it on my left ankle and instep.

And the Hug that you sent me for my knee or should I say knees (I've been alternating) feels terrific. My knees have never been embraced before and I love the feeling. It's far more desirable than an elastic bandage. Incidentally, you sent me the right size—large.

Thank you again, Mr. Wagner. Because of my satisfaction I'm telling a lot of people. In fact, I have given my catalog to a massage therapist I know and would like another one....

> Sincerely, Paula"

"Hello David,

Thanks for your info. So, let's see how we organize ourselves next time we have an order.

For your customer satisfaction file: For several months I had been under treatment for a frozen left shoulder (due to an accident). In December '98, there still remained an impairment of mobility of about 15%, making certain movements quite painful. Four weeks after treating my shoulder to a daily rub with Panther Juice, I am finally free of pain and have full movement of my arm again. Hurrah!!!

> Love and light to you all and a good hug with my 2 healthy arms,
> Eva Reinermann "

"Dear David,

Almost every day there is something nice I notice about the Tachyonized products. My wife's tension headaches have slowly disappeared. After years and years of looking for a solution, her systems have charged and she is free of pain. A few years ago I did some humanitarian service during an armed conflict between Peru and Ecuador, and in 17 days I treated chiropractically over 2600 soldiers, which included 10 days on the front lines, four of them living in the Amazon jungle, sleeping in the trenches with the soldiers. It left me exhausted. I have tried a lot of things to get charged up again, even ozone therapy, but nothing has taken me as far as Tachyonized products. Sonia and I took advanced Reiki training and there were roses in the room, which began to wilt due to the heat. At the end of the day I put one drop of Panther Juice in the vase and we watched the roses pick up their heads and look happy again. Well ... I couldn't resist. I put two drops in my juice and drank it. That's why I am ordering your wonderful T-water, one for the family and one for a cancer patient. I have curiosity as to what would be the benefits of injecting Tachyonized (distilled) water into a sick person? Has anyone done that? I have no restrictions here in doing that and I feel safe about it. Have you done it in your health center? It seems to me that when I mix Panther Juice with herbal creams they are absorbed better by the patient.

> Dr. Jim"

"Subject: Tachyonized materials effects

What have you experienced with Tachyonized products? I have been an acupressure therapist since 1985. Three years ago I thought I would have to retire because of arthritis pain in my wrists and hands. I even went back to school and got training in another field! Then I discovered Tachyonized wristbands, and I am still doing acupressure, with very little pain, if any. I also sell products to clients with wonderful results. I keep wristbands and Velcro headbands (which can be worn around the neck tucked under your shirt like an ascot) in stock for my clients because they are so good, and they are only $20.00.

More amazing, my friend's 12-year-old daughter was diagnosed with scoliosis (spine curvature), and she started wearing the waist belt at night. The next time she went to the doctor, he told her she was "dramatically improved." He had no explanation for it!"

"A doctor came in for a treatment for a torn thigh muscle. He limped into the office. I used Tachyonized cells and the procedure for pain relief using the TLC bars learned in the class. After the treatment, he hopped off the table and said.... "I am pain-free!" He climbed the stairs with a spring in his walk and thanked me!

Carol A."

"My husband was injured at work by a falling piece of steel that hit his forehead. When he came home he could not even move his head, the pain was off the scale. Using the TLCs and energy cells, I gave him a treatment. At the end, he was moving his head around and actually probing his head in search of pain!"

"Chronic bursitis in shoulder 90% alleviated!

Lower back pain and weariness gone!! Stress (long-distance travel) does not occur wearing Tachyonized materials! Mats: chronic knee injury—completely healed!"

"Sluggish lymph system improved 90% after treatment. Sore throat and strained voice from intensive singing- does not occur wearing Tachyonized materials!

Donna B."

ABOUT THE
AUTHORS

Gabriel Cousens, M.D., is a holistic physician, psychiatrist, family therapist, Reiki Master, senior Essene teacher, and spiritual facilitator who blends spiritual awareness with the disciplines of nutrition, Ayurveda, naturopathy, homeopathy, and acupuncture in the healing of body, mind, and spirit. He has published scientific papers in the areas of biochemistry, psychopharmacology, school health, and orthomolecular psychiatry.

A graduate of Columbia Medical School, Dr. Cousens is listed in the *Who's Who in California,* and served on the board of trustees of the American Holistic Medical Association.

He is the founder and director of the Tree of Life Rejuvenation Center in Patagonia, Arizona. The Rejuvenation Center is an innovative, rejuvenative, spiritual eco-retreat committed to the integration of all healing life forces for complete body-mind-spiritual renewal. Programs include medically supervised fasts and other detox programs, Pancha Karma (an ancient and powerful Ayurvedic detox and rejuvenation program), Conscious Eating and Living workshops, Zero Point Process (a psychospiritual self-healing training), Reiki levels I, II, and Masters certification, Essene Teachers training programs, organic gardening and live food, apprentice programs. The center provides gourmet kosher vegetarian organic live-food cuisine. You may reach the Tree of Life Rejuvenation Center at 520-394-2520 or e-mail at healing@rejuvenation.com, or visit the center's web site at www.treeofliferejuvenation.com.

Dr. Cousens has been involved in Tachyon research and theory development since 1990. He is certified Quality of One, level one and two, and practitioner course teacher in the United States. Tachyon treatments and courses are available at the Tree of Life Rejuvenation Center. In 1998 Dr. Cousens began assisting David Wagner in the Quality of One, level three, seminars.

In 1985, Dr. Cousens started the Sonoma County Peace 21 Meditation, which he has since taught throughout the world. It was at this time that he met David Wagner and they began their world peace work together. Currently they have begun to create a series of holistic orphanages and spiritually oriented schools, which include holistic health and garden-centered schools located in various regions around the world. Dr. Cousens has also started a Peace 21 Meditation on a quarterly basis at the United Nations in New York, which began in 1995. He is the president of the Global Foundation.

He is the author of four other books: *Spiritual Nutrition and the Rainbow Diet*, *Sevenfold Peace*, and *Conscious Eating*. His latest book, *Freedom from Depression: Activating Your Pleasure Centers* will be released in early 2000.

Dr. Cousens has taught meditation and other courses in university settings, hospitals, mental health centers, hospices, and suicide prevention centers throughout the United States, England, France, Switzerland, Sweden, Germany, Poland, India, Israel, and Costa Rica.

David Wagner was born in 1959 in Torrance, California. Wagner's ancestors migrated to Canada and then to the United States from Germany. His grandparents were Christian missionaries who lived what they taught, ministering for over twenty-eight years in Mexico. Their lives were a spiritual expression of the love, devotion, and compassion of God and they practiced a life free from doctrines while focusing on God's word. This greatly influenced Wagner's childhood, as he spent roughly four months each year with them, living in devotion to God. This allowed him to explore and develop his own inner communication with God and was a keystone to his future inventions and teachings. On the paternal side, Wagner's ancestors have been healers and crystal experts for three generations — a tradition continued by Wagner. At the age of seven, Wagner experienced his first spiritual blossoming as he developed the ability to hear his inner guide, hear people think, and see how energy moves in all of nature.

After Wagner finished his academic studies he took a job working in the budding computer industry, where he specialized in computer-assisted infrared technology and computer diagnostics equipment. By 1983, the field of telecommunications was feeling the effects of the computer revolution, and Wagner quickly became a specialist. His ability to solve problems and create or invent new solutions led to work with satellite communications—he began working for a Fortune 500 company that was introducing the world's first digital switching computer. He also worked with software and hardware, inventing new processes and testing methods, which in turn led to a special privilege with his company.

One of the outcomes was the invention of the W.E.6 and W.E.7 electromagnetic-field processing units. Before he perfected the Tachyonization process, the W.E.7 was considered to be the best neutralizer of EMFs. Later, the Tachyonized silica disks became the world's leading tool for the restructuring and elimination of EMF's harmful effects.

Most of Wagner's inventions were integrated into the companies that employed him. He invented many devices and processors. In 1990, twenty years of research and experiments culminated with the invention of the Tachyonization process, which restructures natural materials at the submolecular level.

Today Wagner is recognized as an accomplished scientist, inventor, entrepreneur, writer, healer, spiritual facilitator of verticality, and peace pilgrim. Wagner has been listed in *Who's Who of America*. He is currently the CEO of Advanced Tachyon Technologies, sits on the board for WholElectric International Inc., is the Vice President of Peace 21, the Commissioner (VP) for the Global Foundation, the director of the Tachyon Health Center, Vice President of the Essene Order of Light Inc., the Vice President of Vertical Living Inc., founder of the Tachyon Institute of Integrated Sciences, and is a global spiritual educator and facilitator.

Wagner developed and is currently teaching three levels of the internationally acclaimed Quality of One workshop and two levels of the practitioner workshop, as well as training and certifying other inspired educators in the Quality of One and practitioner workshops. Wagner routinely teaches in the United States, Europe, and India.

Wagner's continuing evolution in spirituality has led him to explore many paths and philosophies. His spiritual evolution has led him to the clear insight that ultimate divine wisdom and truth can only be found within our own hearts as we wake up, evolve, and embrace our divine connection to all that is.

You may e-mail David Wagner at davidw@planet-tachyon.com. You may reach Advanced Tachyon Technologies at 707-573-5800. You may also visit their web site at www.planet-tachyon.com.